HIGHER

PHYSICAL EDUCATION

Aaron Anderson

Consultant Editor: Jonathan MacWhirter

Boost

HODDER GIBSON
AN HACHETTE UK COMPANY

Every effort has been made to trace all copyright holders, but if any have been inadvertently overlooked, the Publishers will be pleased to make the necessary arrangements at the first opportunity.

Although every effort has been made to ensure that website addresses are correct at time of going to press, Hodder Gibson cannot be held responsible for the content of any website mentioned in this book. It is sometimes possible to find a relocated web page by typing in the address of the home page for a website in the URL window of your browser.

Hachette UK's policy is to use papers that are natural, renewable and recyclable products and made from wood grown in well-managed forests and other controlled sources. The logging and manufacturing processes are expected to conform to the environmental regulations of the country of origin.

Orders: please contact Hachette UK Distribution, Hely Hutchinson Centre, Milton Road, Didcot, Oxfordshire, OX11 7HH. Telephone: +44 (0)1235 827827. Email education@hachette.co.uk Lines are open from 9 a.m. to 5 p.m., Monday to Friday. You can also order through our website: www.hoddereducation.co.uk

© Aaron Anderson 2021
First published in 2021 by
Hodder Gibson, an imprint of Hodder Education
An Hachette UK Company
211 St Vincent Street
Glasgow, G2 5QY

Impression number   5   4   3   2   1
Year   2025 2024 2023 2022 2021

All rights reserved. Apart from any use permitted under UK copyright law, no part of this publication may be reproduced or transmitted in any form or by any means, electronic or mechanical, including photocopying and recording, or held within any information storage and retrieval system, without permission in writing from the publisher or under licence from the Copyright Licensing Agency Limited. Further details of such licences (for reprographic reproduction) may be obtained from the Copyright Licensing Agency Limited, www.cla.co.uk

Cover photo ©WavebreakMediaMicro - stock.adobe.com
Illustrations by Integra Software Services Pvt. Ltd., Pondicherry, India
Typeset by Integra Software Services Pvt. Ltd., Pondicherry, India
Printed in Italy

A catalogue record for this title is available from the British Library.

ISBN: 978 1 5104 8452 8

Contents

	Introduction for teachers	v
	Getting the most from this textbook	v
	What does this textbook do?	v
	Why is the textbook following this approach?	vi
1	**Course structure**	2
	The exam	2
	Practical performance	3
2	**Command words**	5
3	**Factors impacting performance**	9
	Mental factors	11
	Emotional factors	15
	Social factors	19
	Physical factors	23
4	**Data collection**	29
	Methods	30
	Data types	31
	Assessing method suitability	32
	Model performers	44
5	**Feedback**	49
6	**Key planning information**	52
	Analysing data	53
	Goal setting	54
	Principles of training and principles of effective practice	56
	Principles of training	56
	Stages of learning	57
	Principles of effective practice	59
7	**Developing performance**	63
	Approach: mental factors	64
	Approach: emotional factors	68
	Approach: social factors	70

	Approach: physical factors (fitness)	74
	Approach: physical factors (skill)	77
	Approach: physical factors (tactics)	79
8	**Factors impacting performance development**	**84**
	Mental factors	85
	Emotional factors	87
	Social factors	88
	Physical factors	91
9	**Monitoring and evaluating**	**95**
	Monitoring method: training diary	97
	Evaluating method: re-test	99
	Evaluating the effectiveness of a PDP	101
	Identifying next steps	103
10	**Scenario**	**106**
11	**Teachers: putting pedagogical research into practice**	**110**
	Retrieval practice	110
	Co-operative learning	112
	Active learning	116

Revision paper 1	119
Revision paper 2	121
Answers	124
Index	167
Photo credits	170

Introduction for teachers

Getting the most from this textbook

This textbook is designed to help teachers plan, deliver and reflect on their pedagogical practice in the classroom by providing them with a host of teaching and learning strategies that can be used to deliver the theory side of the Higher Physical Education (PE) course.

It will also allow pupils to test and improve their knowledge of the Higher PE course as they work their way through each task before comparing their responses to the Answers section at the back of the book. Pupils can then consolidate and test their knowledge and understanding further by completing the practice papers in the run-up to the exam.

This is not a traditional textbook, in that the learning required for the course is embedded through a multitude of guided discovery tasks that are supplemented with answers at the back to check for progress and understanding. In doing this, pupil's can take ownership of their learning and engage in active learning processes.

What does this textbook do?

This textbook will go through each area of the SQA mandatory knowledge and provide a learning task against each of the five command words in that area. Learners will be asked to identify, describe, explain, analyse and evaluate their understanding in each of the course areas listed below.

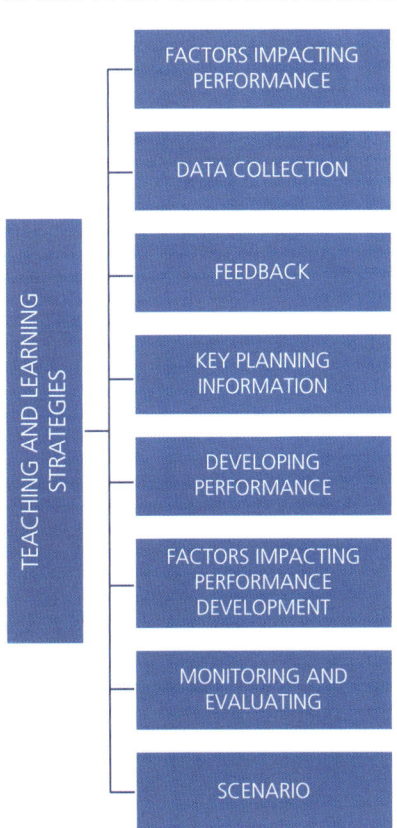

TEACHING AND LEARNING STRATEGIES
- FACTORS IMPACTING PERFORMANCE
- DATA COLLECTION
- FEEDBACK
- KEY PLANNING INFORMATION
- DEVELOPING PERFORMANCE
- FACTORS IMPACTING PERFORMANCE DEVELOPMENT
- MONITORING AND EVALUATING
- SCENARIO

Why is the textbook following this approach?

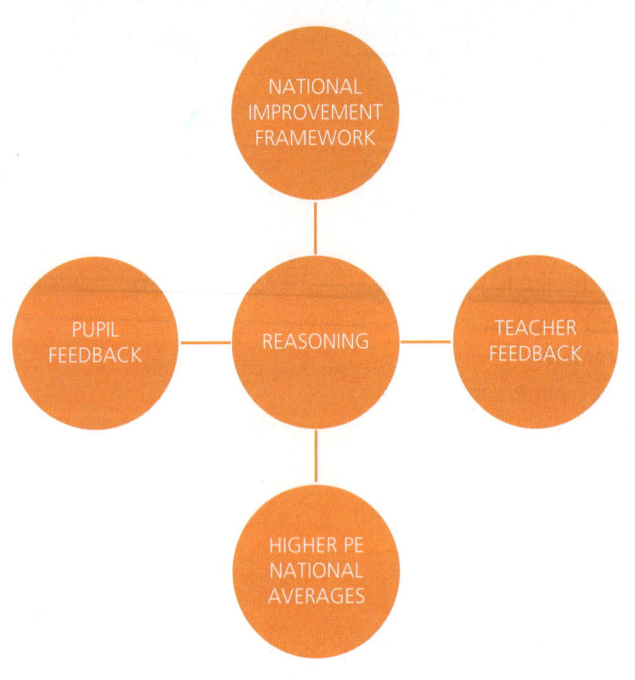

```
            NATIONAL
          IMPROVEMENT
           FRAMEWORK
                |
   PUPIL  ─── REASONING ─── TEACHER
 FEEDBACK                  FEEDBACK
                |
            HIGHER PE
            NATIONAL
            AVERAGES
```

A key driver of the 2020 National Improvement Framework is to develop the literacy skills of learners in and across all subjects.

Two common themes emerged from teacher feedback prior to the publication of this book:

1. Teachers looking for resources to aid delivery of theory-based lessons in a classroom environment.
2. Teachers seeking clarity around the use of command words and strategies for how to answer them in exam-style contexts.

There has been a consistent trend in the Higher PE national averages with the performance element always scoring much higher than the exam element since the inception of the renovated Higher PE course in 2015.

Finally, and most importantly, pupil feedback centred around a lack of confidence in utilising knowledge in theory-based lessons and uncertainty in answering a variety of exam-style questions.

In addressing these key areas, it is hoped that this textbook will improve teacher knowledge and confidence in the classroom, which in turn will lead to more positive learning outcomes for all learners in and through Higher PE.

COURSE STRUCTURE

1 Course structure

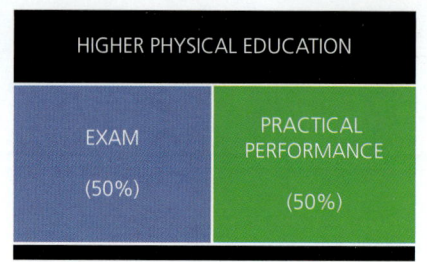

HIGHER PHYSICAL EDUCATION	
EXAM (50%)	PRACTICAL PERFORMANCE (50%)

The Higher Physical Education (PE) course is divided into two components: the theoretical aspect, which is assessed in an end-of-year exam, and the practical aspect, which is assessed in two one-off performances. Each component contributes 50% to your overall grade.

The exam

The end-of-year exam is sat over a two-and-a-half-hour timeframe and is split into three sections, as shown in Figure 1.1.

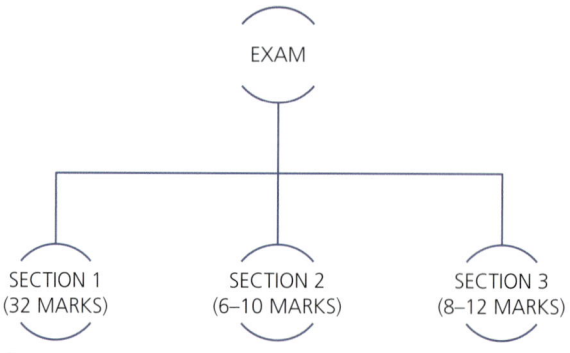

```
           EXAM
    ┌────────┼────────┐
 SECTION 1  SECTION 2  SECTION 3
(32 MARKS) (6–10 MARKS) (8–12 MARKS)
```

Figure 1.1

Section 1 is out of 32 marks. This will test your knowledge on all areas of the mandatory course content. This means you can be asked questions on any of the following:

1. Factors impacting performance.
2. Data collection.
3. Key planning information.
4. Performance development.
5. Monitoring and evaluating.

Section 2 is worth 6–10 marks and will assess your ability to recall how you planned, created and implemented personal development plans (PDPs) in up to two factors.

Section 3 is worth 8–12 marks and comes in the form of a scenario. The scenario is unpredictable and requires you to use your problem-solving skills as you interpret information and use your knowledge to formulate a response.

Practical performance

The practical component of the course contains two one-off performances. In this, your ability to perform in two different practical activities is assessed in a single event. How you do on the day determines your score in each activity. Each performance is scored out of 30, with marks being awarded in the categories shown in Figure 1.2.

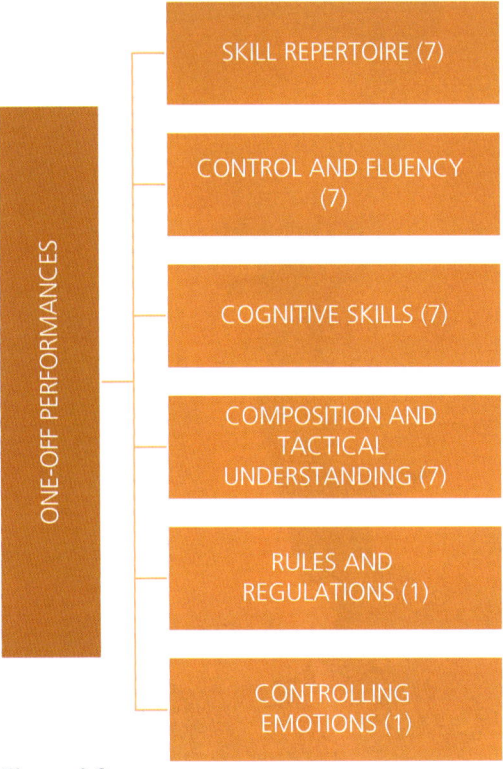

ONE-OFF PERFORMANCES
- SKILL REPERTOIRE (7)
- CONTROL AND FLUENCY (7)
- COGNITIVE SKILLS (7)
- COMPOSITION AND TACTICAL UNDERSTANDING (7)
- RULES AND REGULATIONS (1)
- CONTROLLING EMOTIONS (1)

Figure 1.2

COMMAND WORDS

2 Command words

The exam will test your knowledge in a variety of ways. This is shaped by the **command word** in each question (Figure 2.1). In the Higher course, you are predominantly asked to show your knowledge against five different command words. Each command word has its own rules that you must follow in order to obtain marks.

MY COMMAND WORDS

IDENTIFY	DESCRIBE	EXPLAIN	ANALYSE	EVALUATE
NAME IT!	PAINT THE PICTURE AND PLAY THE VIDEO!	SHOW CAUSE AND EFFECT!	DECONSTRUCT SOMETHING AND GO INTO MINUTE DETAIL!	JUDGE SOMETHING AND PROVIDE EVIDENCE!

Figure 2.1

Identify

An identify question is the most straightforward in the exam: it does not require any sentences as you simply name something.

> **TIP**
>
> Aim for a mark per word or phrase.

> **EXAMPLE**
>
> Identify a qualitative method used to collect data on mental factors. (1)
>
> Questionnaire.

Describe

Describe questions move beyond mere identification. They are asking you to paint a picture inside an examiner's head to show how something looks and is then completed. To help you through this, try to remember the what, who, where, when and how, BUT never the why!

> **TIP**
>
> Aim for a mark per sentence.

> **EXAMPLE**
>
> Describe a quantitative method used to gather information on physical factors. (2)
>
> **Painting the picture:** To complete the bleep test, I placed two cones 20 metres apart on a flat and dry surface in the games hall.
>
> **Playing the video:** At the start of the test, I stood behind one cone and jogged to the other cone 20 metres away on the first bleep, with the aim of reaching it before the next bleep.

Explain

An explain question asks you to give reasons why you chose something or why something happened. In doing this, you need to show cause and effect. *'I chose this because of "X". This meant that "Y" happened.'* Notice how the second sentence starts with the linking phrase 'This meant' – doing this will enable you to bring your cause and effect together.

> **TIP**
>
> Aim for a mark every two sentences.

> **EXAMPLE**
>
> Explain what a performer may consider when setting goals for a social performance development plan. (1)
>
> **Cause:** A performer may consider setting a long-term goal for their social PDP that is realistic to their baseline data collection score.
>
> **Effect:** This means that they will be motivated to give their all in every session as they know improvements are within their reach.

Analyse

Analyse questions relate to the process of something being completed or occurring. To be successful here, you should consider three things:

1. Deconstruct something into important parts.
2. Tell the examiner why this part has been chosen.
3. State the impact of this selected part.

> **TIP**
>
> Aim for a mark every three sentences

> **EXAMPLE**
>
> Analyse an approach used to develop performance in the emotional factor. (1)
>
> **Deconstruct:** It was important that I completed deep breathing at home on my own when doing it for the first time.
>
> **Why:** This was because it freed me from feeling embarrassed or distracted by watching teammates.
>
> **Impact:** This resulted in me fully concentrating throughout the approach and mastering it correctly.

Evaluate

Evaluate questions ask you to look back on something you have completed and judge how effective it was. Once you have made the initial judgement, you must then reinforce this with evidence. Once you have provided this evidence, finish off with the effect it had. This command word refers to the end of the process, so write in the past tense to show the examiner you understand that you are looking back on something that has been completed.

> **TIP**
>
> Aim for a mark every three sentences.

> **EXAMPLE**
>
> Evaluate how effective your performance was in the mental factor after the completion of a personal development plan. (1)
>
> **Judgement:** My concentration levels really improved after completing an effective PDP for the mental factor.
>
> **Evidence:** I know it improved because my score in the performance profiling wheel increased from 2/10 at the start of my PDP to 7/10 in the final re-test.
>
> **Effect:** As a result, it led to me being much more effective when man-marking in basketball as I was better at focusing on my man and intercepting more passes made to them than before my PDP.

Your ability to use the five command words will be tested at the end of each chapter. When completing these tests, you are advised to revisit these pages to help guide your answers.

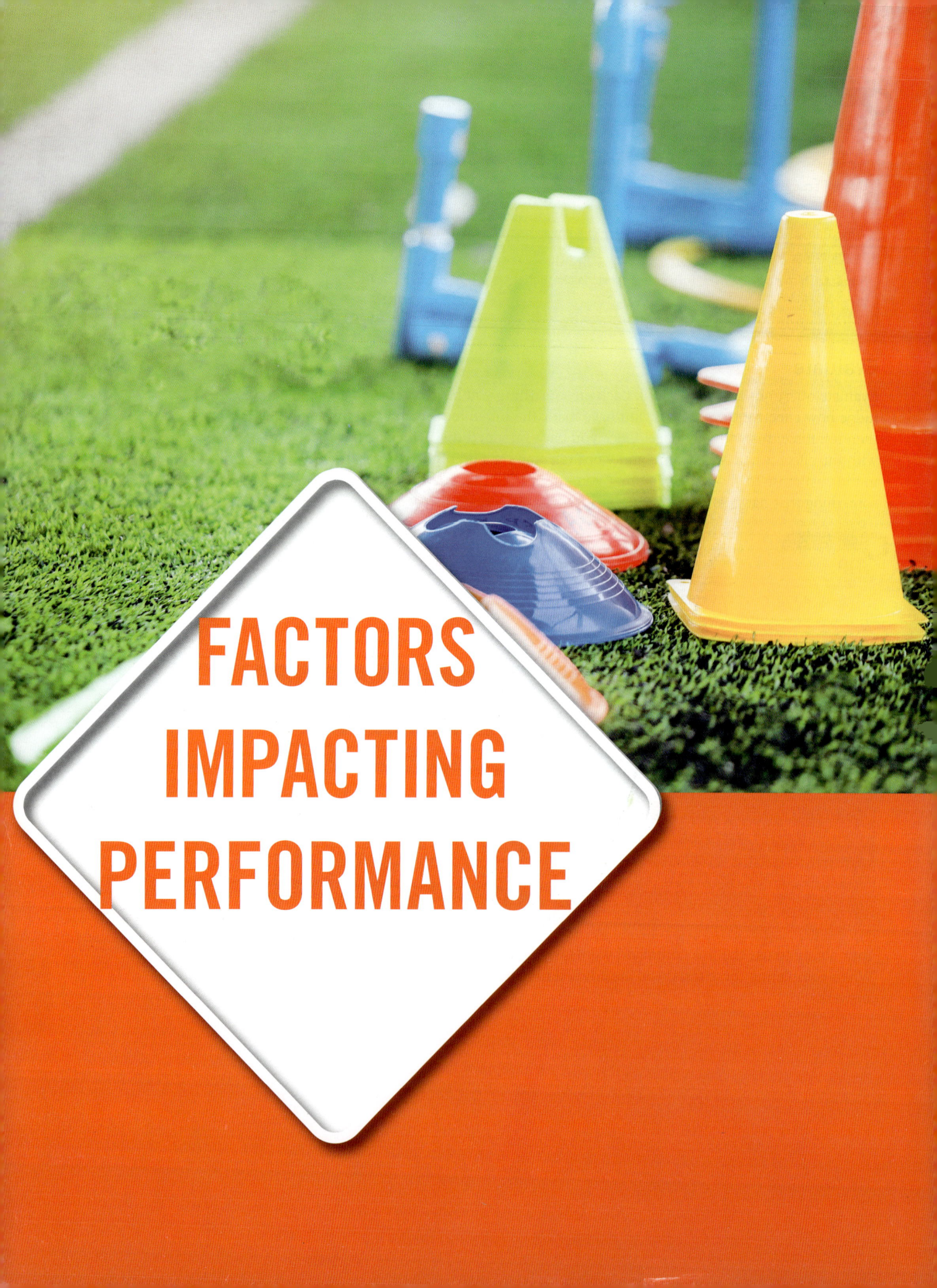

FACTORS IMPACTING PERFORMANCE

3 Factors impacting performance

Four factors lie at the heart of the Higher PE course. Within each factor are 'sub-factors'. It is vital that you understand what factor each sub-factor falls under in order for you to be successful in the exam. The table of factors we will follow in this book can be viewed below.

MENTAL FACTORS ANXIETY CONCENTRATION DECISION MAKING PROBLEM SOLVING	**EMOTIONAL FACTORS** ANGER CONFIDENCE RESILIENCE TRUST
PHYSICAL FACTORS* ACCURACY CARDIO-RESPIRATORY ENDURANCE POWER WIDTH	**SOCIAL FACTORS** COMMUNICATION ETIQUETTE INCLUSION TEAM DYNAMICS

FOUR FACTORS

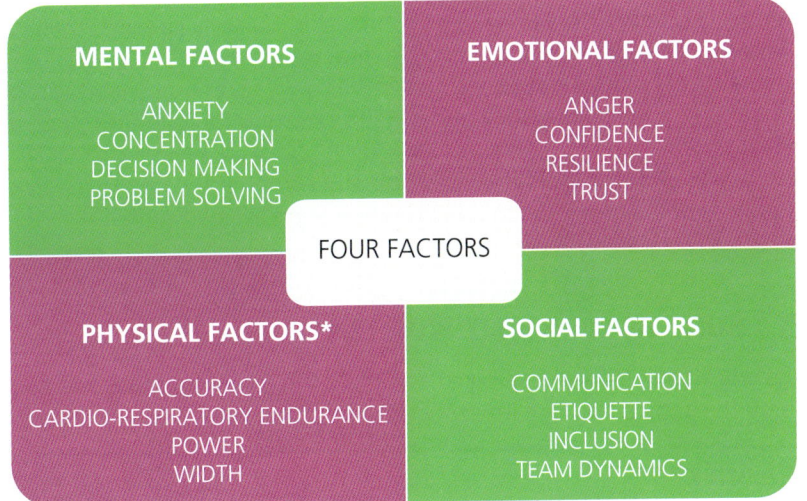

Figure 3.1

*Physical sub-factors can be further divided into skills, fitness and tactics.

When answering questions on factors impacting performance, a good structure to follow is the '3-step process'. Doing this will enable you to be specific whilst also achieving sufficient depth to pick up marks. The three steps are:

1 Specific situation: provide a specific situation within an activity where a sub-factor occurs. Doing this will paint a clear picture in the examiner's head.
2 Impact on performer: now show how the selected sub-factor impacts a performer within this situation. Try to use buzz words (see Task 1) to show your understanding of the sub-factor.
3 Impact on performance: what was then the outcome in this situation? Try to provide a logical outcome here to ensure that your answer stays on the same path throughout.

> ## EXAMPLE
>
> Analyse the impact mental factors could have on performance in an individual activity. (1)
>
> Being mentally tough helped me when I was in the lead on the final lap of my 1500m race. This meant that I never gave up and pushed through the pain barrier as I was starting to tire. This resulted in me maintaining my pace and staying in first position to win.
>
> Let's look at **why** this is a good answer.
>
> 1. Sentence 1 paints a very good picture because it is very specific: the pupil tells us **when** in the 1500m they required mental toughness.
> 2. Sentence 2 uses **buzz words** such as 'never gave up and pushed through the pain barrier' to show that they understand how mental toughness can impact a performer.
> 3. Sentence 3 follows a **logical conclusion** and remains specific to the original situation and the impact of mental toughness on the performer.

TASK 1 SUB-FACTORS BUZZ WORDS

Use the word bank below to help you complete the following table and correctly match up the sub-factor with its associated buzz words.

WORD BANK

chose   tired   frustrated   sportsmanship   bounced back
nervous   called loudly   wings

SUB-FACTOR	BUZZ WORD
Anger	
Communication	
Decision making	
Width	
CRE	
Resilience	
Etiquette	
Anxiety	

OPTIONAL TASK

If you found that too easy, try to create your own buzz words for the remaining sub-factors from our four factors table.

Mental factors

Anxiety

Anxiety is a feeling of uneasiness, nervousness and/or tension that is often brought on in high-pressure situations. Some high-pressure situations you may experience in sporting activities can be found below.

HIGH PRESSURE SITUATIONS
- Serving against a break point in tennis
- Taking a penalty kick in rugby
- Putting to win the tie in golf matchplay
- Performing a dance routine in front of a crowd

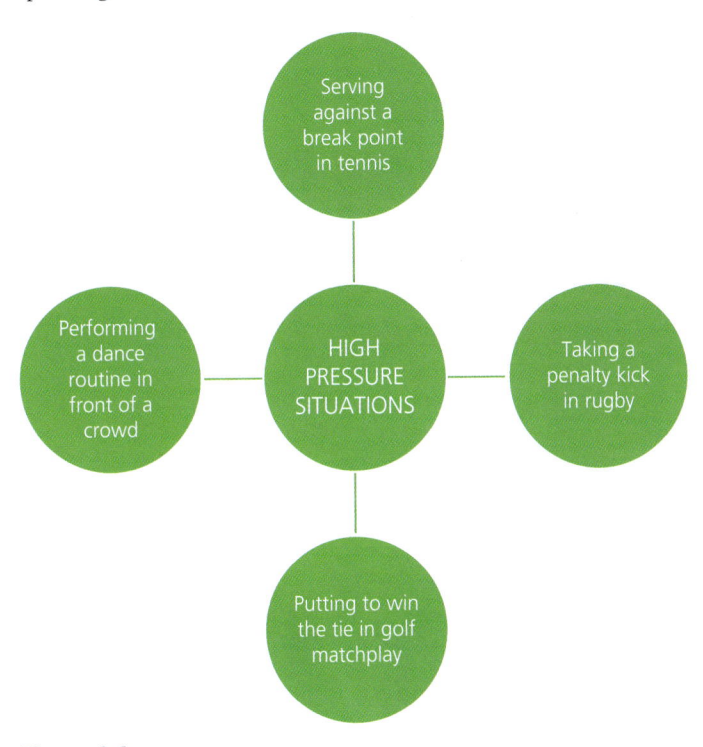

Figure 3.2

Anxiety can impact a performer in two ways: cognitively and somatically:

- A cognitive impact can lead to performers doubting themselves and then losing focus on the task at hand.
- Somatic impacts refer to the physiological responses of the body and include muscle tension, sweaty palms and the shakes.

> **TIP**
> Ensure that your answer follows a logical pattern — sweaty palms are unlikely to impact a rugby player when taking a penalty kick.

> **EXAMPLE**
> I was anxious when I was about to perform my dance routine in front of a large crowd. This meant that I started to worry and my head was full of negative thoughts at the start of my routine. This then caused me to lose my focus and I was out of time with the music.

TASK 2 BUILD THE ANSWER: ANXIETY

Look at the table below and piece each of the three answers together. Remember, the three steps must flow in a logical order.

SPECIFIC SITUATION	IMPACT ON PERFORMER	IMPACT ON PERFORMANCE
I was anxious when serving against a break point in tennis.	This meant the muscles in my legs started to tense up and my movements became rigid.	This resulted in me making a poor connection with the serve which lacked power and hit the net.
I was anxious when taking a penalty kick in rugby.	This meant my body started to shake as I gripped the putter.	This led to me hitting the ball with the wrong part of the putter and my putt missed as it lacked accuracy.
I was anxious when putting to win a matchplay tie in golf.	This meant my palms started to sweat and my grip on the racquet was weak.	As a result, my kick lacked power and missed as it fell short of the posts.

Concentration

Concentration is the ability to focus on what is important in a performance and block out stimuli considered to be irrelevant.

LINKING PE TO LIFE, LEARNING AND WORK

Consider when you have been in class and your teacher is issuing instructions. At the same time as this, your classmate is trying to talk to you. At this point, you have to focus your attention on the teacher and block out your classmate. Doing this will allow you to pick up the instructions clearly and have a higher chance of performing well in the task!

The above school example has many parallels with your practical performance in an activity.

1. When in the games hall playing badminton, there is a high chance that there are other matches taking place on courts around you. You need to focus on the flight of the shuttle on your court and block out the noise from other courts.
2. When man-marking in basketball, there will be other players moving around you on court. You must focus on the person you are marking and not become distracted by the movements of others.

TASK 3 GUIDED DISCOVERY TASK: CONCENTRATION

Pick one of the concentration examples above and provide a **logical and specific** impact on performance.

NOTE: the first two steps have been provided for you with a specific situation and an impact on performer.

Decision making

Good decision-making means making the correct choice when faced with a variety of different options.

In an invasion game such as football, a performer is faced with a range of different situations in which certain decisions must be made. As can be seen below, the decisions a performer faces often depends on their position on the pitch.

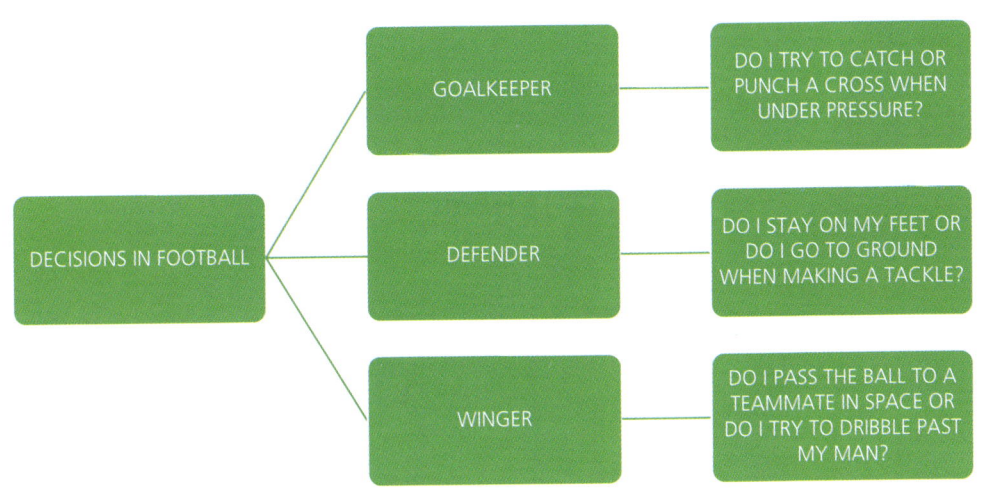

```
DECISIONS IN FOOTBALL
├── GOALKEEPER ── DO I TRY TO CATCH OR PUNCH A CROSS WHEN UNDER PRESSURE?
├── DEFENDER ── DO I STAY ON MY FEET OR DO I GO TO GROUND WHEN MAKING A TACKLE?
└── WINGER ── DO I PASS THE BALL TO A TEAMMATE IN SPACE OR DO I TRY TO DRIBBLE PAST MY MAN?
```

Figure 3.3

> **TIP**
> Show your breadth of knowledge. If you take each of these examples through the 3-step process, you could pick up 3 marks.

As well as this, the decisions a performer may face in football could also be reliant on the score and time in the game. Consider the example below:

> **EXAMPLE**
> I had to decide what to do in football when I was in possession of the ball in the final minute with my team winning 2-1. This meant that rather than go for goal and potentially lose possession, I chose to take the ball towards the corner flag and shield the ball. This resulted in me maintaining possession far away from our goal and running the clock down to help my team see the match out.

The decisions a performer may face in a racquet sport are markedly different to those above. The decisions a tennis player faces often depends on where to place their shot during a rally.

TASK 4 SHOT PLACEMENT: DECISION MAKING

Consider where your opponent ('X') is on the tennis court and do the following…

1. Paint the picture: state the specific situation.
2. Inform the examiner where you would decide to play your shot.
3. Provide a logical conclusion to this rally.

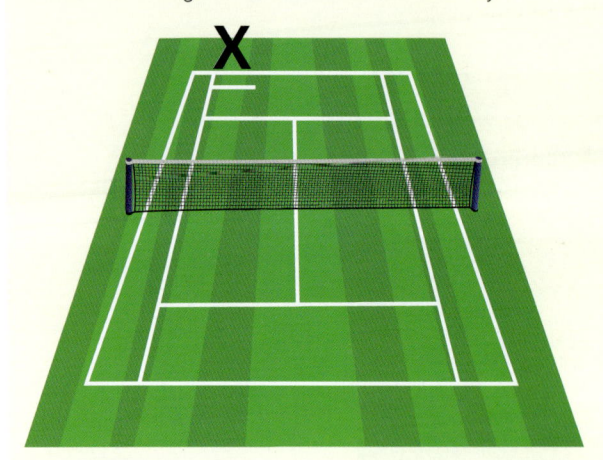

Figure 3.4

Problem solving

Problem solving is the ability to find a solution(s) to a certain problem during a performance.

All activities are dynamic: the state of play is constantly changing and as a result, performers need to think on their feet and overcome any problems that come their way. Consider a golfer who is lining up a putt on the green.

TASK 5 READ THE GREEN

Imagine you are lining up a putt and as you look from the ball to the hole you notice that the green is going up a hill that slants slightly to the left.

1 Work out how you would strike the ball and where you would aim for.
2 Provide a reason for your answer.

What is the likely outcome?

Emotional factors

Anger

Anger is a feeling of frustration that can be caused by yourself, a teammate, the opposition or score.

Returning to breadth of knowledge, a performer can get angry in a range of different situations. This can mostly lead to negative outcomes. Consider this example from handball below.

> **EXAMPLE**
> I failed to control my anger when I was fouled by an opponent in handball. This meant that my frustration boiled over and I lashed out at my opponent in retaliation. This resulted in me being given a two-minute time out and our team having to cover more ground in my absence.

In the example above, a performer has lost their temper due to the actions of an opponent. In Task 6, we will consider how a performer may get angry at a match official and a teammate. In each case, try to fill in the blanks with the most appropriate phrases from the word bank so the answers follow a logical flow.

TASK 6 FILL IN THE BLANKS: ANGER

Use the word bank below to help you complete the following paragraph.

I got angry in basketball after the referee made a call I disagreed with. This meant that I got so frustrated that I started to _____ at them. This resulted in me being _____ and my team playing with one player less.

I also got angry in golf after I missed an easy putt to make par. This meant that I was so angry that I tried to hit my next drive with _____. This resulted in me _____ and it going out of bounds.

WORD BANK

```
ejected from the game    losing control of my shot
far too much force    shout and swear
```

However, in some cases, a performer may be able to control their anger and channel it into a stronger performance.

ANGER WHEN CRITICISED IN NETBALL → CHANNEL ANGER INTO PROVING COACH WRONG → GIVE 100% AND FULFIL POSITIONAL ROLE AND RESPONSIBILITIES TO A HIGH STANDARD

Figure 3.5

Confidence

Confidence means having belief in one's abilities to perform to a high standard in a range of situations.

When a performer is confident, they fully believe in their capabilities and this can have numerous positive impacts on their performance.

A rugby player has the confidence to be creative and throw in a dummy pass to evade an opponent

CONFIDENCE

A football player who is confident will take on a long range shot rather than always playing a sideways pass

Figure 3.6

In each of the above examples, confidence leads to performers taking risks to make their play more unpredictable. In other cases however, the confidence levels of a performer can impact to what extent they commit to an action and whether they hesitate or not. Consider the example from gymnastics below.

> **EXAMPLE**
>
> A gymnast who is high in confidence will demonstrate their belief in their run up to the springboard when vaulting. This means that they will fully commit to their run-up and perform it at a high speed. This results in them building up momentum and power which aids their take off from the springboard and generates more height from which they can perform a high-quality somerrsault.

TASK 7 BE THE EXAMINER: CONFIDENCE

Read this pupil's answer on a lack of confidence when serving in volleyball. Consider how we use the 3-step process and provide them with feedback on each sentence on why that sentence was good or how their sentence could be improved.

1 Feeling low in confidence negatively impacted me when taking a serve in volleyball.
2 This meant that I did not believe in myself.
3 This resulted in my shot hitting the net.

TIP

When writing a positive and negative answer for one sub-factor, do NOT flip your answer. Consider different contexts to get around this.

Resilience

Resilience is the ability to bounce back and move on after a mistake has been made.

Being resilient is key to success in PE, education and life. Everybody makes mistakes but it's the ability to bounce back from these setbacks and learn from them that will determine how successful you are.

CASE STUDY

Sporting example

During the 10,000m final at the 2016 Olympic Games, Sir Mo Farah demonstrated resilience after falling early in the race. Rather than giving up, he bounced back quickly and forgot about the mishap to switch his focus back on to the race. As a result, he caught up with his competitors and regained his pace quickly to retake the lead and win gold.

Figure 3.7

When writing out an answer on resilience, *the specific situation given in sentence 1 should always be about a mistake or a negative that happened.* By being specific here, it will enable you to remain specific in the remainder of your answer as you discuss how you managed (or did not manage) to move on.

> **TASK 8 PERSONALISED RESILIENCE ANSWER**
>
> Consider an activity you will be assessed in as part of your one-off performances. From this, do the following:
>
> 1 Identify a mistake you may make in your performance.
> 2 Be positive and talk about how resilience can help you personally after this error.
> 3 Finish it with what you would then do in the performance.

Consider the example from netball below to help guide your answer:

> **EXAMPLE**
>
> I will show my resilience if I miss a shot whilst playing goal attack in netball. This means I will forget about the miss and continue to make attacking runs into the shooting circle. This will result in me having other opportunities to score without being affected by my previous miss.

> **LINKING PE TO LIFE, LEARNING AND WORK**
>
> Consider when you put your hand up to answer a question in English. The teacher selects you and you answer incorrectly. If you lack resilience, you will feel embarrassed and dwell on this mistake rather than offer your answers again. Without answering again, it is difficult for you or the teacher to identify what stage you are at in your learning.

Trust

Trust is the extent to which you believe in and rely on your own abilities as well as those of your teammates.

If a performer really trusts their teammates to fulfil their own role and responsibilities to the best of their abilities, it will help them focus on their own performance.

Consider a striker in football. If they fully trust that the winger will beat their opponent and deliver a cross into the box, then the striker will make runs across the front of defenders to get into space for a chance to score. However, if the striker does not trust the winger to do this, they will stop making these runs which could be detrimental should a cross actually come in.

TASK 9 TRUSTING MY TEAMMATES

Consider a dancer who is performing in a national event with their group. In practice, one of their teammates has been consistently out of time and has, unfortunately, showed no signs of improving.

Use your knowledge of the 3-step process to demonstrate the impact a lack of trust could have on their performance.

Figure 3.8

Social factors

Communication

Communication means verbally and non-verbally interacting with teammates during a performance.

A team that displays high levels of communication are likely to be well organised and efficiently functioning as opposed to a team that does not talk. Like other sub-factors, communication is used in a variety of different situations across a range of different activities.

- Alerting a teammate in possession that you are in space and free for a pass
- Shouting your name to alert your doubles partner that you will play the shot
- Calling 'man on' to make your teammate aware that an opponent is running behind them to make a tackle

Figure 3.9

Consider the badminton example below and what would happen if there was no communication.

> **EXAMPLE**
>
> Failing to communicate negatively impacted my performance in a doubles badminton match when the shuttle was about to land between me and my partner. This meant that with no one communicating we were both confused as to who would play the shot and left it for each other. As a result, nobody attempted to return the shuttle and we lost an easy point.

TASK 10 COLOUR CODE: COMMUNICATION

Grab two different highlighter/coloured pens and colour-code each of the three steps below to coordinate two new communication answers.

Communicated when setting the ball up to teammate in volleyball.	Shouted the direction for the team to move in as the opponents passed the ball.	My teammate was ready and set to perform an accurate spike.
Communicated when organising our zonal defence in handball.	Shouting my teammate's name to alert them to the incoming pass.	Stayed unified and moved as a unit to minimise gaps for opponents to shoot.

Etiquette

Etiquette means displaying sportsmanship as you follow the unwritten rules of an activity.

Demonstrating high levels of etiquette is a choice that you make. It is not an official rule and cannot be punished by match officials if not shown. It does however lead to increased respect between you and the opposition.

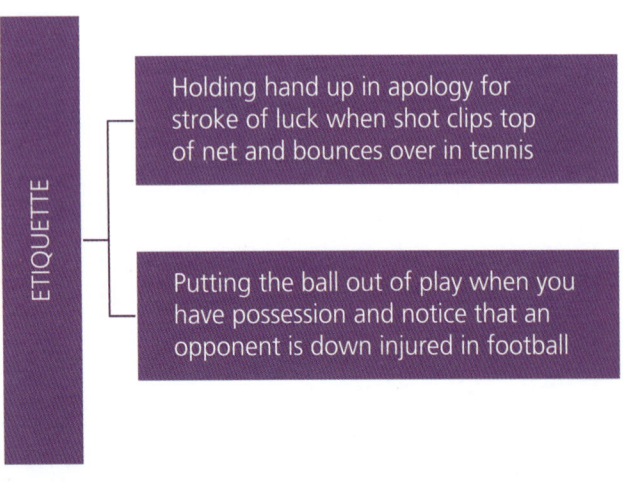

ETIQUETTE
- Holding hand up in apology for stroke of luck when shot clips top of net and bounces over in tennis
- Putting the ball out of play when you have possession and notice that an opponent is down injured in football

Figure 3.10

CASE STUDY

Sporting example

Rafael Nadal showed high levels of etiquette when an opponent's serve was incorrectly called out in tennis. This meant that he sportingly pointed out to the umpire the ball mark in the clay to prove that his opponent's serve actually landed in. This resulted in the respect between the two players growing and the match being played in a fair manner.

Figure 3.11

TASK 11 ETIQUETTE EXAMPLES

1. Identify two different sporting situations from those above in which an athlete may demonstrate etiquette. Remember, this is a sporting action they choose to make rather than something they must do.
2. Pick one of these situations and talk through the impact on both the performer and then the performance. You may use the Rafael Nadal example to guide you.

Team dynamics

Team dynamics refer to how well teammates within a team get along with each other and support one another in good and bad moments.

Teams who have high levels of chemistry amongst them are more likely to be successful than those who do not as they work hard for one another to help achieve the groups aims.

TEAM DYNAMICS		
Encouraging a teammate after they miss a conversion kick in rugby	Covering for a teammate when they are out of position in handball	Supporting a teammate against a tricky opponent to make it a 2 vs 1 in football

Figure 3.12

In each of the above examples, the consistent theme is that team dynamics can really come to the fore when a teammate is struggling. Consider this for the football example below.

> **EXAMPLE**
>
> Good team dynamics helped our teammate in football when he was facing a tricky winger. This meant one of our teammates supported him to create a 2 against 1 in their favour. As a result, they managed to stop the winger getting past them and dispossessed them to regain possession for our team.

TASK 12 SUB-FACTOR PINBALL: TEAM DYNAMICS

In some cases, demonstrating high levels of team dynamics can pinball on to some mental and emotional sub-factors.

1. Identify 3 sub-factors from the mental and/or emotional factors that can be impacted in this basketball example.
2. Pick one and take it through the 3-step process.

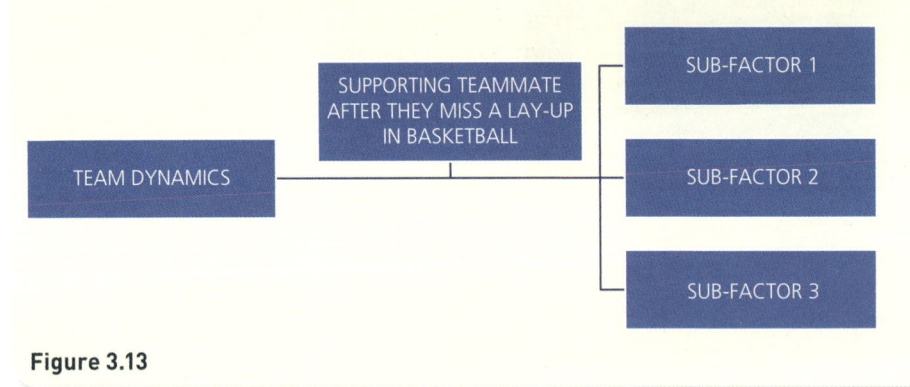

Figure 3.13

Inclusion

Inclusion means involving every team member in performances and enabling them to feel valued by others.

It is very important that all members of a team feel included before, during and after a performance. The diagram below shows how others may feel included and therefore valued.

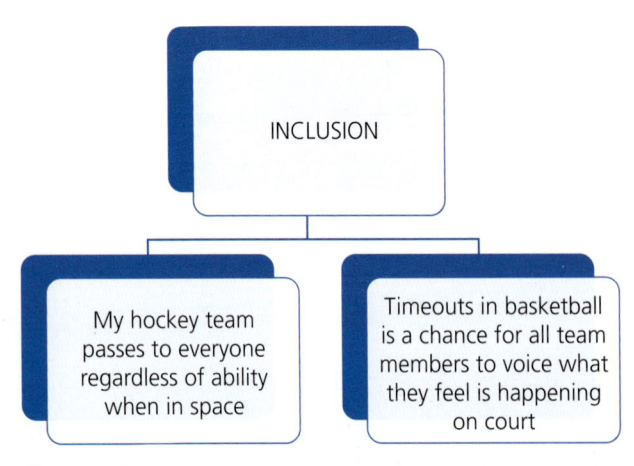

Figure 3.14

TASK 13 FEELING EXCLUDED

Finish off the 3-step process based upon the specific situation provided.

1. A lack of inclusion negatively impacted our team when we were attacking up the court in handball.
2. This meant that two of our teammates only ever passed to each other despite a number of us being in good positions.
3. This resulted in …

Physical factors

Accuracy

Accuracy means being precise and hitting a designated target when executing skills and techniques.

When performing a range of different skills, it is important that you execute them accurately. Being accurate brings a multitude of different benefits to your performance.

A hockey player who can make an accurate pass can maintain possession for their team

A tennis player who can perform a drop shot accurately will drop the ball just over the net and put their opponent under pressure

ACCURACY

A volleyball player who can perform an accurateset can tee up teammate to perform a spike with little to no adjustment

A golfer who can accurately putt will have a better short game and produce a lower score to be in with a chance of winning tournaments

Figure 3.15

Likewise, a performer who inaccurately performs a variety of skills and techniques would see a reduction in their effectiveness. Complete Task 11 below to consolidate your knowledge on accuracy.

TASK 14 MATCH-UP: ACCURACY

1. Match up the situation and negative impact in the table below.

Inaccurate dig in volleyball	Ball does not go far enough into the corner and is close to the goalkeeper who saves it.
Inaccurate shot in hockey	Ball does not follow a straight line and goes off to the side and lands out of bounds.
Inaccurate lob in tennis	Ball goes behind teammate and out of play for a point to the opposition.
Inaccurate drive in golf	Ball is hit with too much power and lands out at the back of the court.

2. Pick a positive example from a different activity in the diagram above and take it through the 3-step process.

Cardio-respiratory endurance (CRE)

Cardio-respiratory endurance (CRE) is the ability of the heart and lungs to work together to pump oxygenated blood to the muscles for a long period of time during exercise.

A performer's CRE levels really come into play in the final moments of an activity. When writing the specific situation in sentence 1, it is useful to reference the time in the performance, such as:

- Final set of a badminton match.
- Second half of a rugby match.
- Last mile in a marathon.
- Last quarter of a basketball match.

Like other sub-factors, writing about CRE can be very beneficial because it has so many different impacts. Learning a variety of these impacts can really help you achieve a breadth of knowledge that can enable you to pick up multiple marks.

- Cannot keep up with pace of play
- Reduction in skill level
- Loss of concentration
- Decision making decreases

Figure 3.16

TASK 15 PRACTICE QUESTION: CRE

Consider this question below:

'More errors are observed, especially towards the end of the live performances.'

Analyse the possible impact of physical factors on the live performances. (4).

Although other physical factors can be referred to here, there are four marks available and we have identified four potential impacts CRE can have on performance. Look at the example answer below and take one of the other impacts identified above through the 3-step process in an activity of your choice.

More errors could have been observed in the final set of a badminton match because the performer had low CRE levels. This meant that they were so tired they started to lose focus and were not tracking the flight of the shuttle as well as they previously were. As a result, their timing was out and they made more unforced errors, losing cheap points.

Width

Width is the horizontal distribution of players to create space on the pitch/court for others.

To maximise the effectiveness of an attack, a tactical consideration a coach is likely to make is how to create width. A coach can do this through the formation they decide to use and the instructions they provide to their players.

In both of the above cases, staying wide creates space in the centre of the pitch/court as it causes opponents to spread out to try and nullify attacks. Doing this then opens up 'pockets' for creative players to operate in and create chances for teammates.

However, in some cases in football, even though a winger may be asked to stay wide, their predominant foot may be opposite to the side they are on. This causes them to cut inside, removing the width and leading to play being congested.

WIDTH

A handball coach will instruct their wingers to stay wide to the touchline

A football coach may instruct full backs to make overlapping runs to create width

Figure 3.17

TASK 16 SPOT THE DIFFERENCE: WIDTH

Below are two answers — can you compare and contrast them to…

1 Identify the better answer.
2 Provide reasons why your selected answer is better.

Answer A
Using width in was really helpful for our team's performance in a recent handball match. This meant our wingers stayed wide to create space for others.

Answer B
Having our wingers stay wide to the touchline was really helpful in a handball match. This meant they stretched the play and caused spaces to open up in the centre of the court. This resulted in our pivot getting into spaces and shooting.

Power

Power is a combination of speed and strength that leads to you performing actions explosively.

Power is used in a variety of different activities as can be viewed below.

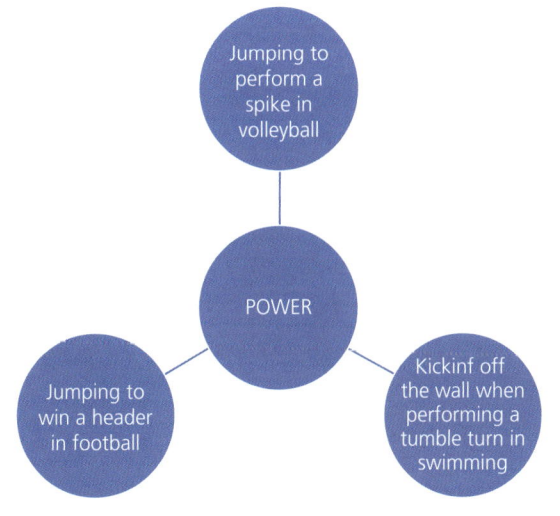

- Jumping to perform a spike in volleyball
- POWER
- Jumping to win a header in football
- Kickinf off the wall when performing a tumble turn in swimming

Figure 3.18

CASE STUDY

Sporting example

Figure 3.19

Cristiano Ronaldo is famed for his ability to jump and tower above defenders when heading the ball. This is underpinned by the power in Ronaldo's legs, enabling him to jump with so much force that he is propelled upwards. This results in Ronaldo scoring a lot of headed goals because he can get higher than defenders to win the ball and score.

TASK 17 PICTURE PERFECT

Look at the picture on the right and write a 3-step process answer that refers to the positive impact power can have in a performance!

Figure 3.20

CHAPTER SUMMARY

The Higher PE course contains four factors:
1 Mental
2 Emotional
3 Social
4 Physical

In each factor are a range of sub-factors that can have both positive and negative impacts on performance. In the physical factor, these sub-factors can be further divided into:

A Fitness
B Skills
C Tactics

Some tips to follow when answering questions on factors impacting performance are below.

TIPS

3-STEP PROCESS: specific situation, impact on performer, impact on performance

NEVER FLIP AN ANSWER: if giving a positive and negative example of the same sub-factor, use different contexts and/or activities to steer clear of contradicting yourself

BREADTH OF KNOWLEDGE: as we have discovered, many sub-factors occur in different ways across activities. Show this breadth of knowledge to help you obtain more marks

Figure 3.21

EXAM-STYLE QUESTIONS

1 Explain the impact mental factors could have on performance. (2)
2 Analyse the impact social factors could have on performance. (2)
3 Analyse how an emotional factor could impact a physical factor. (1)

TIP

Regardless of the command word in factors impacting performance questions, always follow the 3-step process.

DATA COLLECTION

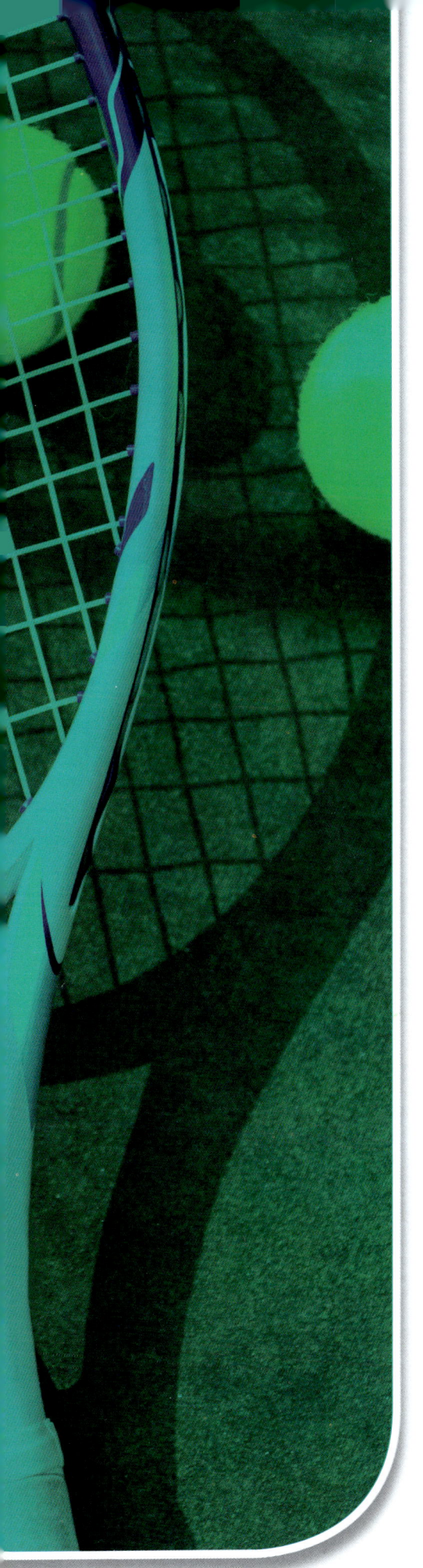

4 Data collection

Having learned about the factors that lie at the heart of the Higher PE course, it is now time to take each of them through a process called the cycle of analysis (Figure 4.1).

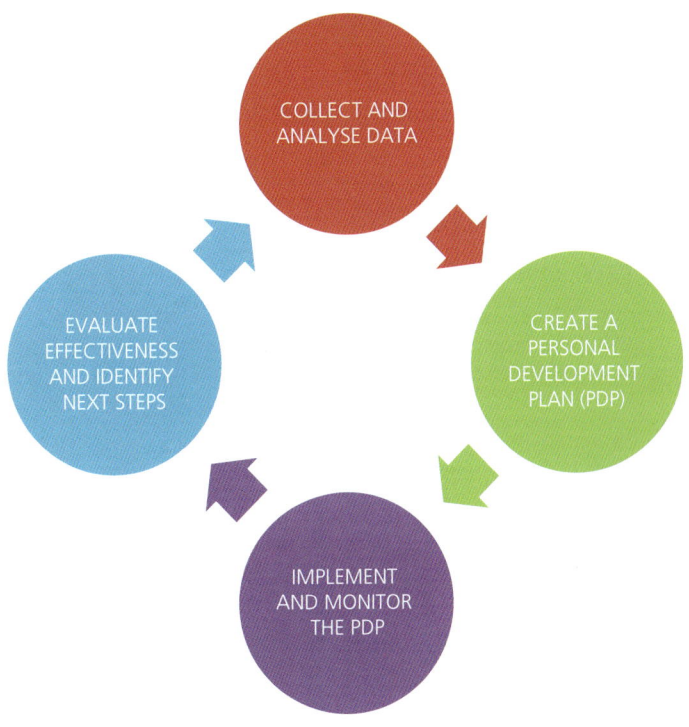

Figure 4.1

At the very start of the cycle, a performer needs to collect data on their performance levels in each factor. This data collection and analysis process involves investigating and researching the strengths and weaknesses of certain selected 'sub-factors'. Figure 4.2 shows why a performer should collect and analyse data before starting a personal development plan (PDP).

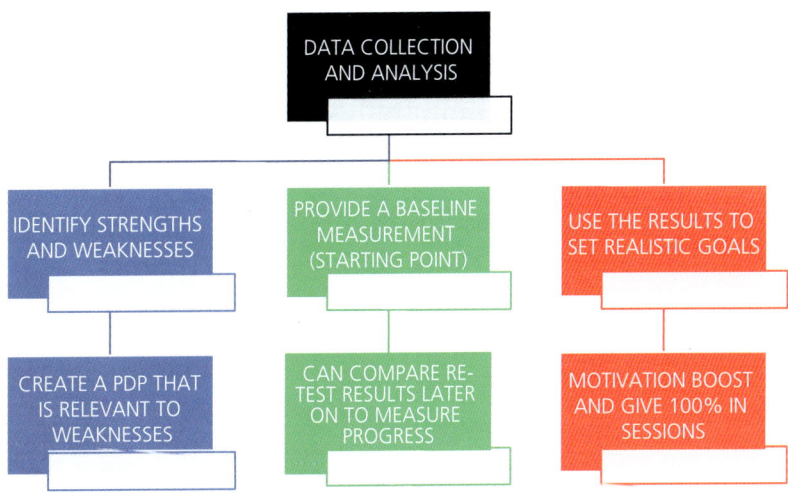

Figure 4.2

> **LINK**
> You will explore PDPs in Chapter 6: Key planning information.

Methods

When collecting data on a factor, a performer will use what is known as a method of data collection. As can be seen in Table 4.1, there are many different types of data collection method.

Mental	Emotional	Social	Physical fitness	Physical skill	Physical tactics
Sport competition anxiety test (SCAT)	PPW	Questionnaire	Standardised fitness test*	PPW	Knowledge of results
Questionnaire	Profile of mood status (POMS) test	Communication observation schedule*	Time-related observation schedule	General observation schedule*	Coach feedback
Decision making observation schedule	Questionnaire*	Coach feedback	PPW	Focused observation schedule	Digital analysis*
Performance profiling wheel (PPW)*	Disciplinary record with video analysis *	PPW	Heart rate monitor	Scatter diagram	Match analysis

*The methods highlighted are the methods that will be focused on in this book.
Table 4.1

The method a performer selects is dependent on numerous variables:

- the 'sub-factor(s)' they are interested in
- the activity they participate in
- the classmates they can work with – for example, is there someone with the expertise to observe them and complete a method accurately?
- the facilities available to the performer.

Note: You only need to know two different data collection methods per factor.

It is important that you can apply each of the command words to your selected methods.

> **TIPS**
>
> You cannot do two examples of the same method. For example, you cannot do the bleep test and the Illinois agility test as both are standardised fitness tests.
>
> Methods such as the PPW can be used for all factors. Minimise the amount you need to learn and achieve depth.

Data types

Different methods of data collection produce different types of data. This is due to the way in which they are completed and the results they produce. There are two types of data: qualitative and quantitative. Each of these data types sits at either end of a continuum.

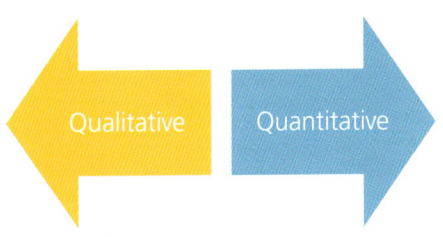

Figure 4.3

Qualitative data

This type of data involves a personal opinion and is subjective in nature. It can be very useful to gather this type of data when investigating mental and emotional factors as only a performer truly knows how they feel. An example of a method that produces qualitative data is a questionnaire. Some of the reasons why a performer should collect qualitative data can be seen in Figure 4.4.

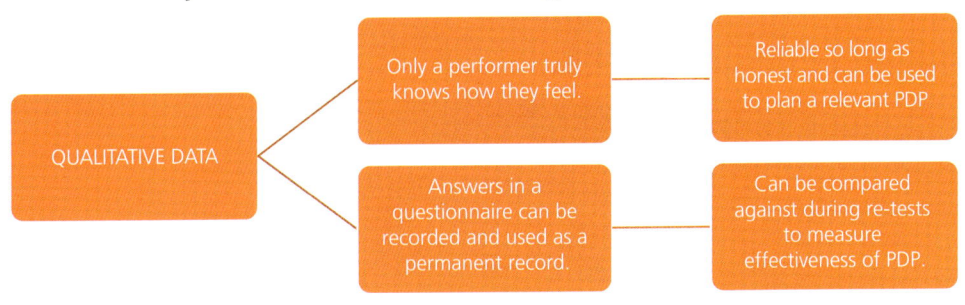

QUALITATIVE DATA
- Only a performer truly knows how they feel.
- Reliable so long as honest and can be used to plan a relevant PDP.
- Answers in a questionnaire can be recorded and used as a permanent record.
- Can be compared against during re-tests to measure effectiveness of PDP.

Figure 4.4

Quantitative data

This type of data is more factual and includes a score being attributed to the end result. It can be very useful in terms of accuracy and reliability. An example of a method that produces quantitative data is a standardised fitness test. Some of the reasons why a performer should collect quantitative data can be seen in Figure 4.5.

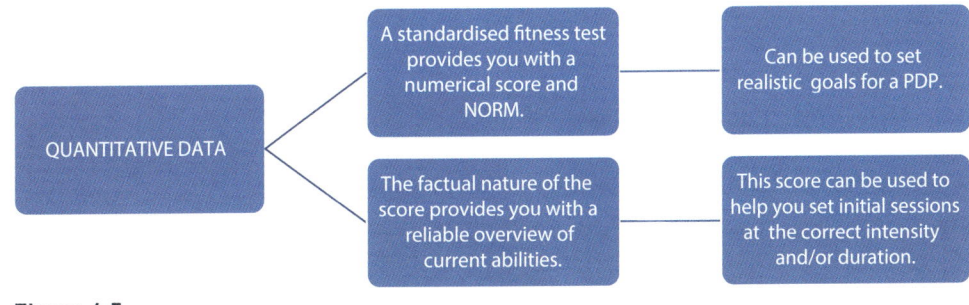

QUANTITATIVE DATA
- A standardised fitness test provides you with a numerical score and NORM.
- Can be used to set realistic goals for a PDP.
- The factual nature of the score provides you with a reliable overview of current abilities.
- This score can be used to help you set initial sessions at the correct intensity and/or duration.

Figure 4.5

However, not all methods are placed at either end of the continuum. A performance profiling wheel (PPW, see p XXX), for example, is qualitative. Even though it produces a score, the score is based upon the opinion of the performer. It can be made more quantitative, though, by combining the method with video analysis. This would involve a performer watching their performance back and then completing the PPW after it. Therefore, there are elements of opinion being based on what actually happened and was observed.

> **TASK 18 CLOSED READING: DATA TYPES**
>
> Having read the above, answer the questions below.
>
> 1 Identify a qualitative method of data collection for the emotional factor. (1)
> 2 Explain why a performer may wish to collect qualitative data when investigating their performance in the emotional factor. (1)
> 3 Identify a quantitative method of data collection for the physical factor. (1)
> 4 Explain why a performer may wish to collect quantitative data when investigating their performance in the physical factor. (1)

> **TIP**
>
> Since 'explain' questions are only worth one mark each, you only need to provide one matching cause and effect.

Assessing method suitability

When selecting which method to use, you ultimately want to assess how useful it is in helping you investigate your performance levels in each factor. An acronym you can use to do this is PARV(M) (Figure 4.6).

PRACTICAL
- Is the method easy to use?
- Would it be easy to identify my strengths and weaknesses from the results?

APPROPRIATE
- Does the method actually collect data on the 'sub-factor' I am interested in?
- Does the method come with norms established by sports science research, such as the bleep test?

RELIABLE
- Does it provide me with accurate results that I can trust?
- Are the protocols of the method used the same way everywhere across the world?

VALID
- Can I defend the process of completion?
- Consider: location, observant others, level of opposition, time of completion, comprehension of questions, amongst other variables.

MEASURABLE
- Is the method a permanent record?
- Can it be looked back on at a later date?

Figure 4.6

TASK 19 STICKY NOTES: PARV(M)

Create a table with a heading for each of the letters in PARV(M). Place each sticky note in the correct column.

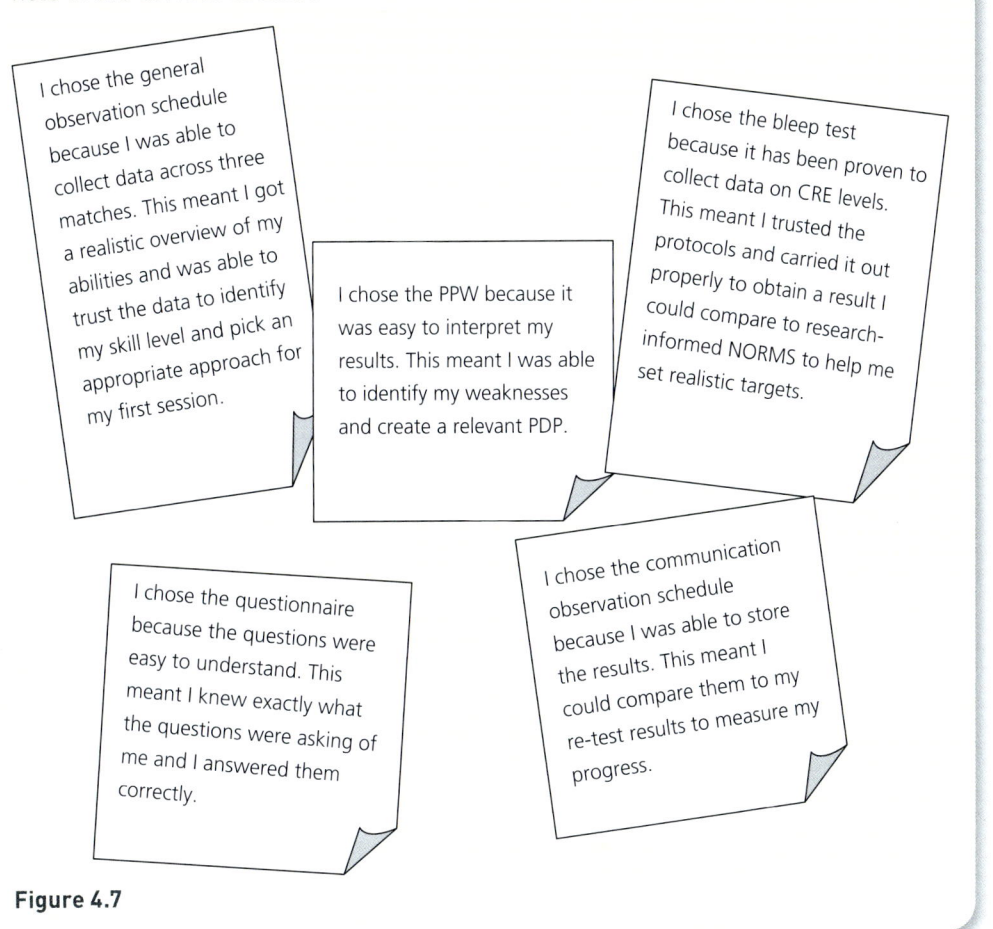

I chose the general observation schedule because I was able to collect data across three matches. This meant I got a realistic overview of my abilities and was able to trust the data to identify my skill level and pick an appropriate approach for my first session.

I chose the PPW because it was easy to interpret my results. This meant I was able to identify my weaknesses and create a relevant PDP.

I chose the bleep test because it has been proven to collect data on CRE levels. This meant I trusted the protocols and carried it out properly to obtain a result I could compare to research-informed NORMS to help me set realistic targets.

I chose the questionnaire because the questions were easy to understand. This meant I knew exactly what the questions were asking of me and I answered them correctly.

I chose the communication observation schedule because I was able to store the results. This meant I could compare them to my re-test results to measure my progress.

Figure 4.7

Method of data collection: mental factors

Performance profiling wheel

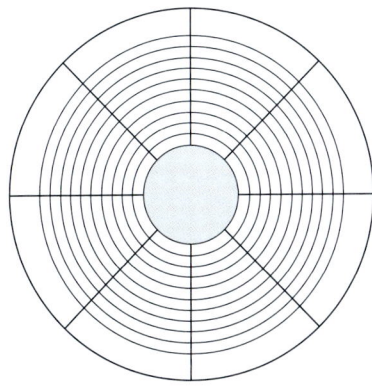

Figure 4.8

The PPW can be used for any factor because you place the appropriate 'sub-factors' on the outside of each section. It is qualitative in that you score yourself out of 10 based on your opinion of your abilities. Let's look at this method in relation to our five command words.

TASK 20 THE PPW AND COMMAND WORDS

1 Identify a method used to collect data on mental factors. (1)

Having identified our method, let's consider how it looks. Your aim here is to create a picture in the examiner's head so they can see the PPW. Pretend they have never seen this method before and be specific. We will start you off…

The PPW is a circle containing eight sections with a mental 'sub-factor' placed around the outside of each section.

2 Describe one other feature of the PPW. (1)

Now that we have painted the picture, we need to give the examiner clear instructions on how this method is completed. It is useful to do this in a chronological order.

3 CLOSED READING: read the following paragraph and bullet-point each descriptive point. (3)

I completed the PPW at home on my own with all electronic devices turned off. I considered my score out of 10 in a mental 'sub-factor' and shaded in the appropriate number of segments. I then repeated this for each of the other 7 mental 'sub-factors' and identified my highest and lowest scores.

Having described our method of data collection, let's now consider some of its benefits and limitations.

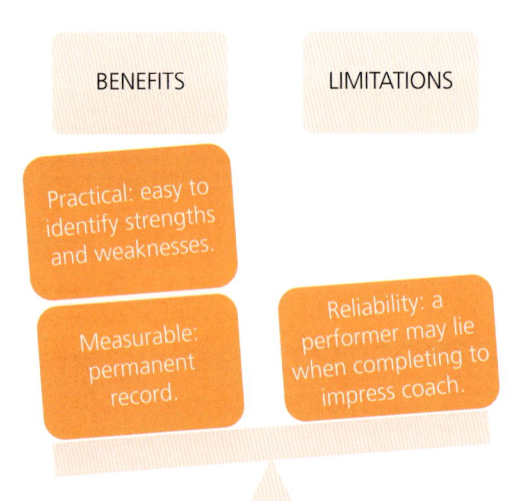

BENEFITS
- Practical: easy to identify strengths and weaknesses.
- Measurable: permanent record.

LIMITATIONS
- Reliability: a performer may lie when completing to impress coach.

Figure 4.9

4 Referring to the benefits of the PPW, can you now **explain** why this method could be chosen? (2)

5 In regard to the limitation of the PPW, can you **evaluate** one way that it could be ineffective? (1)

Let's finish by looking at an aspect of what makes the PPW work. In doing this, we are analysing this method of data collection.

6 GUIDED DISCOVERY: **analyse** one other important part of this method of data collection.

Pick one of the deconstructed parts below and provide a reason why that part is important AND the impact it then has on the data collected.

- Complete the PPW the same day of a performance.
- Ask a coach to check over your results (particularly on decision making).

Complete the PPW at home on your own. — DECONSTRUCT

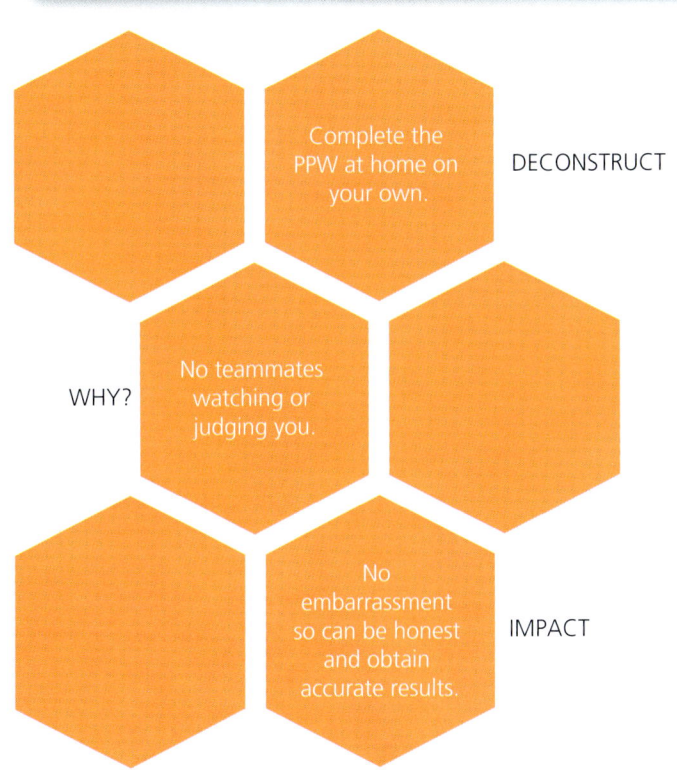

WHY? — No teammates watching or judging you.

No embarrassment so can be honest and obtain accurate results. — IMPACT

Figure 4.10

Method of data collection: emotional factors

Questionnaire

	Not at all	A little	Moderately	Quite a bit	Extremely
Uneasy	0	1	2	3	4
Upset	0	1	2	3	4
Exhilarated	0	1	2	3	4
Irritated	0	1	2	3	4
Pleased	0	1	2	3	4
Tense	0	1	2	3	4
Sad	0	1	2	3	4
Excited	0	1	2	3	4
Furious	0	1	2	3	4
Joyful	0	1	2	3	4
Nervous	0	1	2	3	4
Unhappy	0	1	2	3	4
Enthusiastic	0	1	2	3	4

	Not at all	A little	Moderately	Quite a bit	Extremely
Annoyed	0	1	2	3	4
Cheerful	0	1	2	3	4
Apprehensive	0	1	2	3	4
Disappointed	0	1	2	3	4
Angry	0	1	2	3	4
Energetic	0	1	2	3	4
Happy	0	1	2	3	4
Anxious	0	1	2	3	4
Dejected	0	1	2	3	4

Table 4.2

An example of a questionnaire used to collect data on emotional factors is the sport emotion questionnaire. This questionnaire contains 22 emotive terms that are split into 5 different categories: anxiety, dejection, excitement, anger and happiness. You must consider the extent to which you feel each emotion during a performance and give it a score from '0: not at all' to '4: extremely'.

TASK 21 THE QUESTIONNAIRE AND COMMAND WORDS

1. Identify a method used to collect data on emotional factors. (1)
2. True/False: below are four descriptive statements placed in a randomised order. Go through each of them and consider whether they would be true or false. For those that are false, correct them. (4)
   a. This questionnaire has 19 emotive terms split into 5 different categories.
   b. You would complete this questionnaire at home on your own with all electronic devices turned off.
   c. You would consider the extent to which you feel each emotion during a performance and rank it from 1 to 5.
   d. You would complete this questionnaire three days after a performance.
3. MATCH UP: in Table 4.3 are three causes and effects that explain why a performer may use this questionnaire. Can you match them up? (3)

CAUSE	EFFECT
I chose the sport emotion questionnaire because it was practical as it was easy to complete.	This meant the memories of my performance were fresh in my head and I was able to accurately complete the questionnaire.
I chose the sport emotion questionnaire because it was valid as I was able to complete it on the day of my performance.	This meant I was able to compare my baseline results with my re-test results to see if I was improving during my PDP.
I chose the sport emotion questionnaire because it was measurable as it was a permanent record.	This meant I made no mistakes in an easy process and my answers were correct.

Table 4.3

When evaluating any aspect of the course, it is important to show both the benefits and limitations. However, it is vital that you do not contradict yourself. For example, if you spoke about the method being effective because you found it easy to complete and it gave you accurate results, you cannot then talk about it being ineffective because you lied and so your results were not accurate.

4 **PROBLEM SOLVING:** consider the following limitation of this questionnaire. Can you then place it beside a benefit in Table 4.3 that ensures there is no evaluative contradiction? (1)

> The sport emotion questionnaire was ineffective because it was hard to understand some of the emotive terms. This was limited because I was unsure what the term meant and simply guessed my response. As a result, my answer to this emotive term was inaccurate.

TIPS

To get around this, write the PARV(M) acronym down the side of your question paper. From here, place a tick next to the letter you consider to be a benefit and a cross next to the letter you consider to be a limitation. Now consider your answer: am I writing something in the cross that contradicts the tick? This will help you plan your answer before you write it.

To overcome this limitation, we can put in place a solution that would make the process more robust. Doing this shows you are analysing the process.

5 **FILL IN THE BLANK:** analyse why this part has been identified as being an important part to completing the questionnaire. (1)

DECONSTRUCT: have access to a dictionary as you complete the questionnaire. → **WHY:** FILL IN THE BLANK. → **IMPACT:** this will help you provide a more accurate score as you know what the emotion is.

Figure 4.11

Method of data collection: social factors

Communication observation schedule

FORM OF COMMUNICATION	YES	NO
VERBAL: asking for a pass.		
VERBAL: shouting own name when going to claim a 'loose ball'.		
VERBAL: calling 'man on'.		
VERBAL: organisational shout: zone defence.		
NON-VERBAL: pointing to where you want to receive a pass.		

Table 4.4

The communication observation schedule comes in the form of a table with a variety of communication forms in the left column. In the observation schedule in Table 4.4 are some of the different verbal and non-verbal communications used in handball. A performer would hand it to a knowledgeable classmate who would observe your performance and place tallies in the appropriate box. The observation should take place against opposition of similar ability across three different games. At the end of the process, strengths and weaknesses of the performer's communication skills should be noted down.

TASK 22 THE COMMUNICATION OBSERVATION SCHEDULE AND COMMAND WORDS

1. Identify a method used to collect data on your performance in the social factor. (1)
2. BE THE EXAMINER: go through the following describe answer and identify areas that could be improved. For each area selected, provide feedback on how to improve the answer. (2)

> I used the communication observation schedule to collect data on my communication skills in handball. The communication observation schedule was a table with different forms of communication in the left column and two further columns with yes and no to the right. I would pick any classmate available to watch my performance and tally whether I did or did not perform each form of communication. I would have them do this across three games because it makes my data reliable as it rules out a 'fluke' performance. At the end of the process, they would give me feedback on my strengths and weaknesses.

There are many reasons why a performer would choose to use an observation schedule to collect data on social factors.

3. GUIDED DISCOVERY TASK: Figure 4.12 gives some of the reasons why a performer would choose to use an observation schedule. Can you now provide the effect to each of the 'causes' given? (3)

EXPLAINING WHY: THE COMMUNICATION OBSERVATION SCHEDULE

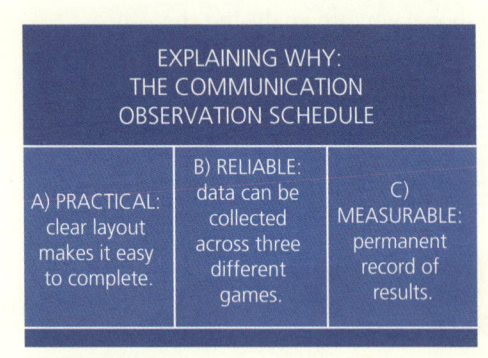

| A) PRACTICAL: clear layout makes it easy to complete. | B) RELIABLE: data can be collected across three different games. | C) MEASURABLE: permanent record of results. |

Figure 4.12

However, despite these reasons for using the communication observation schedule, a major limitation of this method is that it can be hard to tell who is talking, so the accuracy of the data could be questioned.

4. TAKE YOUR PICK: pick one of the limitations below and evaluate why it could negatively impact on the data collected. (1)
   a. Play against opposition who are too good for your team.
   b. Time consuming collecting data across three different games.
5. BUILD THE ANSWER: piece together the answer parts in Table 4.5 to build two analytical answers.

DECONSTRUCT	WHY	IMPACT ON DATA
Combine the observation schedule with digital analysis.	Understand what each form of communication looks/sounds like in the context of the activity.	Fill out the table correctly to provide a more accurate overview of your strengths and weaknesses.
Have a knowledgeable partner observe your performance.	Overcome the fast-paced nature of the game to ensure nothing is missed.	Get the full picture of performance, which increases the reliability of results.

Table 4.5

Method of data collection: physical factors (fitness)

Standardised fitness test

Figure 4.13

Standardised fitness tests are used to assess fitness levels in a variety of physical 'sub-factors'. The T-Test measures one's agility; the press-up test measures a performer's muscular endurance and the bleep test their CRE levels. As we are focusing on CRE as part of the physical factor, we will look at the bleep test in more depth.

> **TASK 23 THE STANDARDISED FITNESS TEST AND COMMAND WORDS**
>
> 1 Identify a quantitative method used to collect data on physical factors. (1)
> 2 DRAW THE PICTURE: based on Figure 4.13, can you describe how the bleep test is set up? (1)

Figure 4.14 shows some other considerations around how to set up and complete the bleep test.

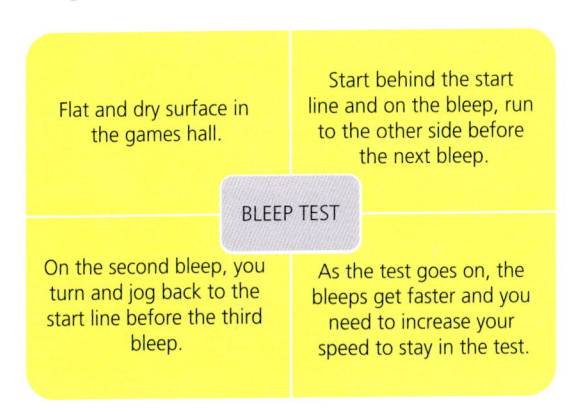

BLEEP TEST
- Flat and dry surface in the games hall.
- Start behind the start line and on the bleep, run to the other side before the next bleep.
- On the second bleep, you turn and jog back to the start line before the third bleep.
- As the test goes on, the bleeps get faster and you need to increase your speed to stay in the test.

Figure 4.14

> 3 RESEARCH: a pupil has said that they are *out when they miss any two bleeps during the bleep test*. Research this online to provide feedback on why this descriptive point is incorrect. (1)

4 **MIND MAP:** Figure 4.15 shows a mind map a pupil has started that helps them explain why they used the bleep test. Some of their answers have a cause and others have an effect. Fill in the missing boxes to help them complete the task. (3)

- A.
- Practical: easy to identify my CRE levels.
- Reliable: provided me with a quantitative score.
- B.
- This meant I was able to compare my baseline and re-test results to see if I had improved.
- C.

Explain why you decided to use the bleep test to collect data on physical factors. (3)

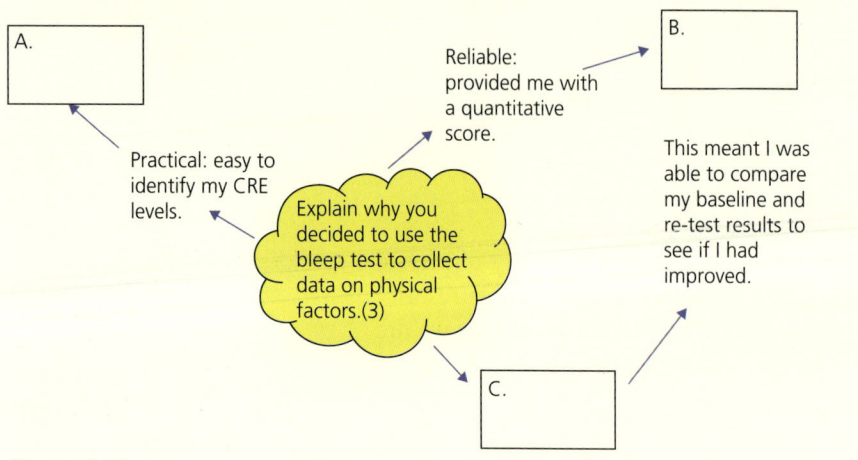

Figure 4.15

> **TIP**
> When answering an explain question, ask yourself 'so what?' after you have written the cause to help guide you into the effect.

5 **DIGGING DEEPER:** despite it being known that the bleep test provides you with a quantitative, figurative score, can you evaluate how the score achieved can actually be unreliable and therefore limited? (1)

6 There are numerous aspects a performer must consider when completing the bleep test to ensure it is as valid and reliable as possible. In Figure 4.16, number the six different stages to show two analytical answers that follow the process of: deconstruct – why – impact. (2)

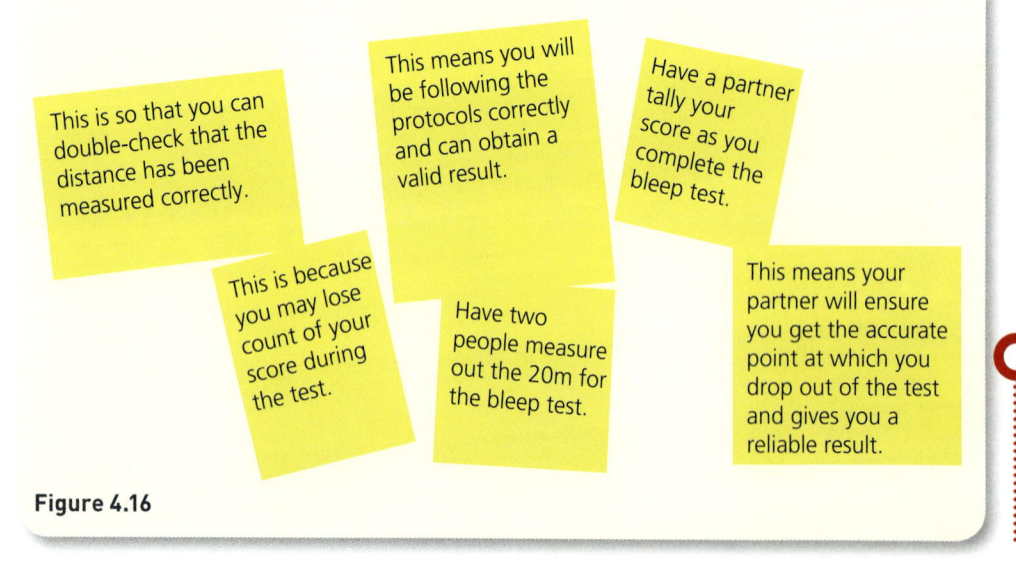

- This is so that you can double-check that the distance has been measured correctly.
- This means you will be following the protocols correctly and can obtain a valid result.
- Have a partner tally your score as you complete the bleep test.
- This is because you may lose count of your score during the test.
- Have two people measure out the 20m for the bleep test.
- This means your partner will ensure you get the accurate point at which you drop out of the test and gives you a reliable result.

Figure 4.16

> **TIP**
> Consider the people around you when doing the bleep test.

Method of data collection: physical factors (skill)

General observation schedule (GOS)

	HIGH SERVE	LOW SERVE	OVERHEAD CLEAR	UNDERARM CLEAR	DROP SHOT	SMASH
EFFECTIVE						
INEFFECTIVE						

Table 4.6

The GOS is used to assess the accuracy and consistency of a performer's skill repertoire. Table 4.6 shows an example of a GOS used in badminton; however, it can be adapted to include the skills and techniques from multiple other activities such as football, basketball and volleyball. The process of completion is very similar to the way the communication observation schedule is completed, so we will now go through Task 24 with reduced guidance in comparison with other sections of this book to test your ability to recall and adapt information.

TASK 24 THE GOS AND COMMAND WORDS

1 Identify a method used to collect data on physical factors. (1)
2 COMPLETE THE DIAGRAM: In Figure 4.17 there are four sections: the look, who, when and how. Complete each area to the best of your ability to help you describe the GOS. Note: the number next to each term indicates how many descriptive points are required in each area. (5)

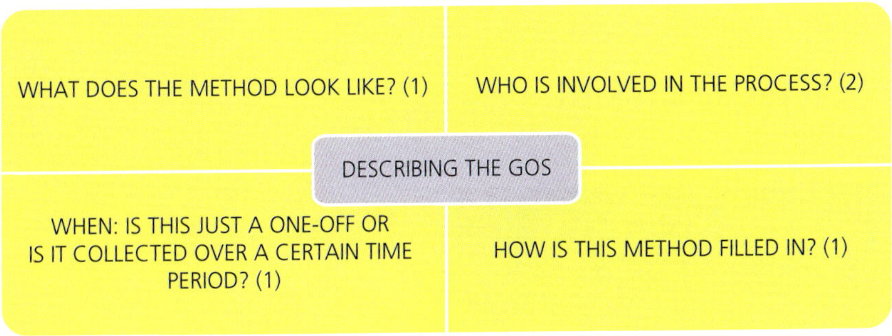

WHAT DOES THE METHOD LOOK LIKE? (1)	WHO IS INVOLVED IN THE PROCESS? (2)
WHEN: IS THIS JUST A ONE-OFF OR IS IT COLLECTED OVER A CERTAIN TIME PERIOD? (1)	HOW IS THIS METHOD FILLED IN? (1)

DESCRIBING THE GOS

Figure 4.17

> **TIP**
>
> LOCK AND KEY: when writing out an explain answer, it is important that the cause and effect you include in your answer fits together. Consider this like a lock and key. The cause is the lock and the key the effect. If the key fits in the lock, you open up a mark.

3 In this task, you need to read a pupil's explain answer, then rewrite it so that each of their causes and effects fit together. (3)

I chose the GOS because it was practical as it was easy to interpret my results. This meant that I was able to show my 'normal' performance levels as I took on a challenge I would normally face and this gave a realistic overview of skill levels in badminton.

I also chose the GOS because it was practical as it was easy for my partner to complete. This meant I was able to identify my strongest and weakest skills, then create an appropriate PDP to improve my weakness.

Finally, I chose the GOS because it was valid as I played against an opponent who had similar levels of ability to mine. This meant they made no mistakes in an easy process and the data I received was accurate and correct.

4 BENEFITS AND LIMITATIONS: create a table with two headings: Benefits and Limitations. Evaluate the answers in Figure 4.18 and place them in the correct column. (4)

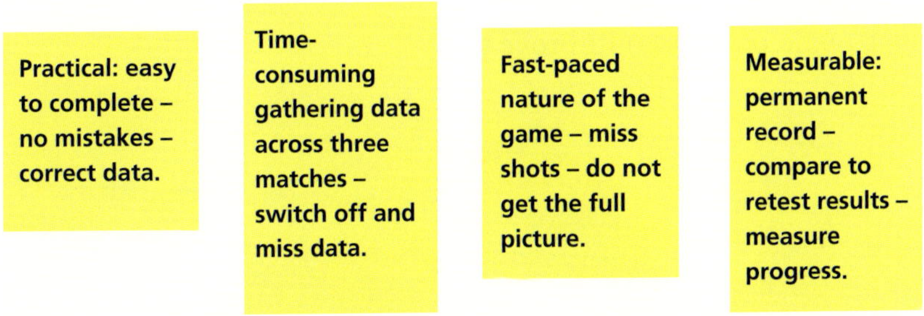

> **TIP**
>
> When writing out your explain answer, try to have a paragraph for each cause and effect. This will help keep your work organised and make it easier for you when re-reading your answers at the end of the exam to see if you have achieved the marks available.

| Practical: easy to complete – no mistakes – correct data. | Time-consuming gathering data across three matches – switch off and miss data. | Fast-paced nature of the game – miss shots – do not get the full picture. | Measurable: permanent record – compare to retest results – measure progress. |

Figure 4.18

4 Data collection

41

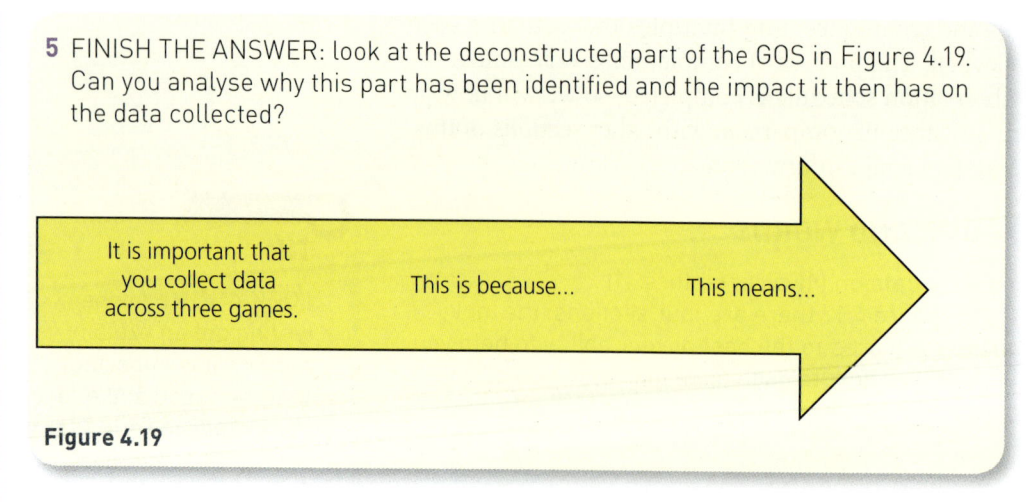

5 **FINISH THE ANSWER:** look at the deconstructed part of the GOS in Figure 4.19. Can you analyse why this part has been identified and the impact it then has on the data collected?

It is important that you collect data across three games. This is because... This means...

Figure 4.19

Method of data collection: physical factors (skill)

Digital analysis

Figure 4.20

A quantitative method used to collect data on the tactics a team employs is digital analysis. This is when a team's performance is recorded on a video and certain aspects of their play are analysed by the coach. In relation to the content in this book, the coach may be looking at how width is achieved during a fast break in basketball to create and exploit space. Based on what is seen on the video, feedback can be given and plans made on how to improve the performance.

TASK 25 DIGITAL ANALYSIS AND COMMAND WORDS

1 Identify a quantitative method used to collect data on physical factors. (1)
2 DELETION: look at each of the descriptive points below and delete the 'weaker' response, leaving you with three correct descriptive answers. (3)
   - The iPad was placed at the side of the games hall at ground level on the centre line. VERSUS The iPad was placed high up on a stand at one end of the games hall.
   - A match against a team of similar ability level was recorded on the iPad. VERSUS A match against a team of lesser ability was recorded on the iPad.
   - After the match, the coach watched the video alone and provided the team with verbal feedback on their strengths and weaknesses. VERSUS After the match, the coach watched the video and provided the team with verbal feedback on their performance as they showed them when the strengths and weaknesses occurred.

Using digital analysis as a means of collecting data on a performance comes with multiple benefits and limitations.

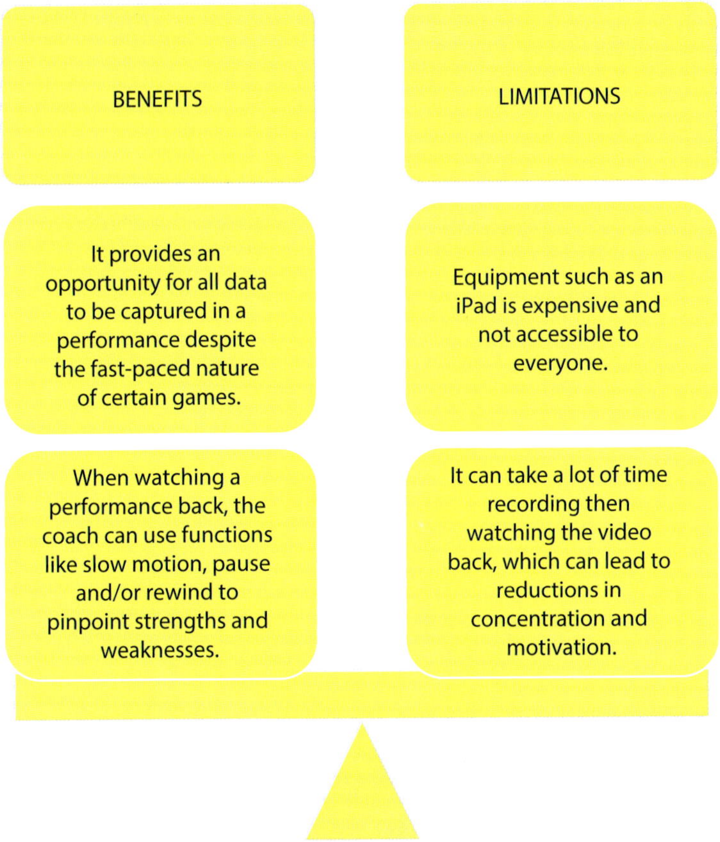

BENEFITS

- It provides an opportunity for all data to be captured in a performance despite the fast-paced nature of certain games.
- When watching a performance back, the coach can use functions like slow motion, pause and/or rewind to pinpoint strengths and weaknesses.

LIMITATIONS

- Equipment such as an iPad is expensive and not accessible to everyone.
- It can take a lot of time recording then watching the video back, which can lead to reductions in concentration and motivation.

Figure 4.21

> **TIP**
> Figure 4.21 does not fully provide causes and effects. Build on this to write enough to pick up 1 mark.

Using Figure 4.21 to help you, can you answer the following questions?

3 Explain why a performer may use this method to collect data on physical factors. (1)

4 A Higher PE pupil has placed an initial judgement of 'slightly effective' on digital analysis. Use this judgement to help guide you to build a 2-mark evaluate answer. (2)

Having considered some of the benefits and limitations of digital analysis, let's analyse an important part to carrying out this method correctly.

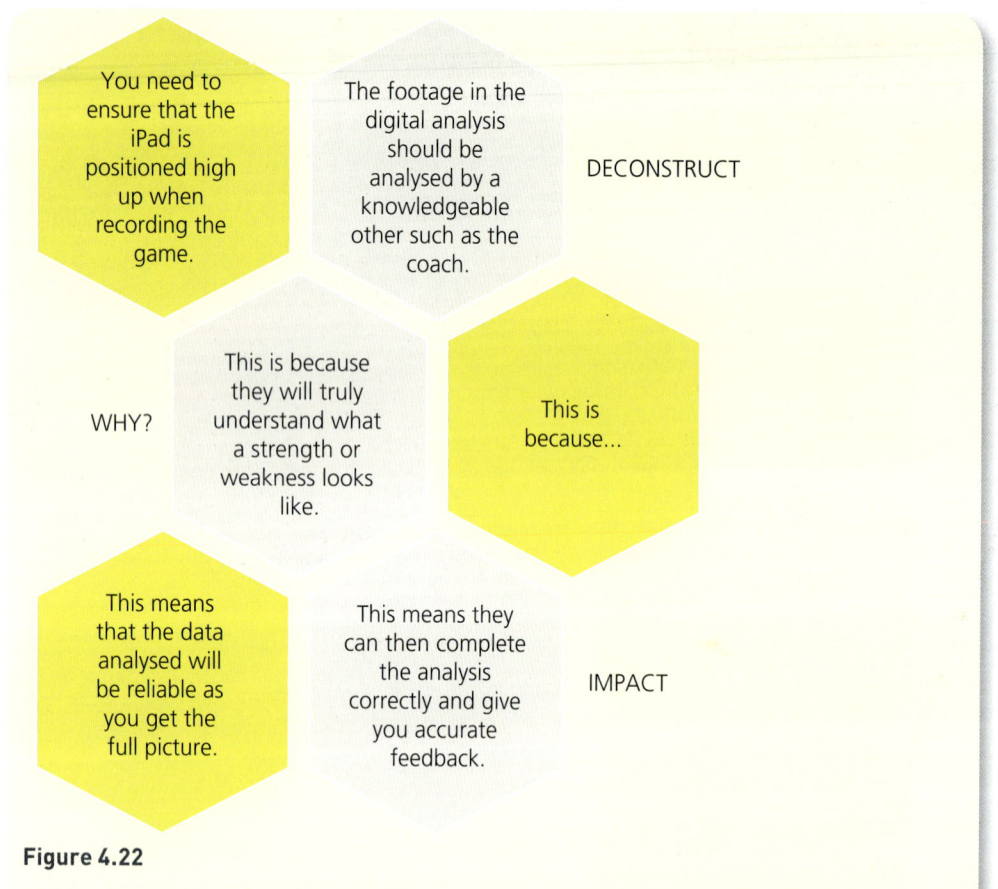

DECONSTRUCT
- You need to ensure that the iPad is positioned high up when recording the game.
- The footage in the digital analysis should be analysed by a knowledgeable other such as the coach.

WHY?
- This is because they will truly understand what a strength or weakness looks like.
- This is because…

IMPACT
- This means that the data analysed will be reliable as you get the full picture.
- This means they can then complete the analysis correctly and give you accurate feedback.

Figure 4.22

5 FILL IN THE BLANK: the yellow pathway is missing the 'why' of the analyse answer. Look at the deconstruct and impact parts of the answer to help guide you in writing an answer for the 'why'. (1)

You may also look at the grey analyse answer to help you with the structure.

Model performers

A model performer is someone who demonstrates a consistently high standard of performance in their activity. In regard to the Higher PE course, we can consider certain athletes to be model performers in each factor. This is because you are unlikely to find one athlete who excels in all four factors. When collecting data, we may compare our performance levels with those of a model performer. A data collection method that does this is the focused observation schedule, where a model performer's sub-routines are listed and compared.

CASE STUDY

Figure 4.23

Mental: Simone Biles consistently shows excellent levels of concentration and has managed to control her anxieties in a range of high-pressure situations.

Emotional: Lionel Messi is consistently fouled yet always controls his anger. He also exudes confidence in taking risks and shows resilience to continue taking penalty kicks despite missing previously.

Social: Tom Brady is known to be an excellent organiser when setting up and carrying out set plays in his role as a quarterback. His communication skills allow him to excel here and have led to him being named as captain on numerous occasions.

Physical: Serena Williams demonstrates great levels of power in her performance as a tennis player. She allies this with an exemplary high skill level and broad repertoire that sees her execute skills with both accuracy and consistency.

TASK 26

Evaluate your performance levels in a factor of your choice in comparison to a model performer. (2)

> **TIP**
>
> When answering this question, it is vital that each 'sub-factor' you refer to contains a comparison of what a model performer does and what you then do. Support this with evidence from the performance. For example:
>
> Like a model performer, my agility levels are of a very high standard when attacking in basketball. This means that like a model performer, I am able to fake to go one way and quickly change direction to go the other way to get past my opponent into space.

A model performer does not have to be an elite athlete, however. This is because a performer may lose confidence in their abilities when comparing themselves with someone of such a high standard, as they ultimately fall below that level. Other examples of model performers that you may compare your abilities with are:

- classmates
- team captains.

As Figure 4.24 shows, there are many reasons why an appropriate classmate may be chosen as a model performer, as referred to during the data collection stage.

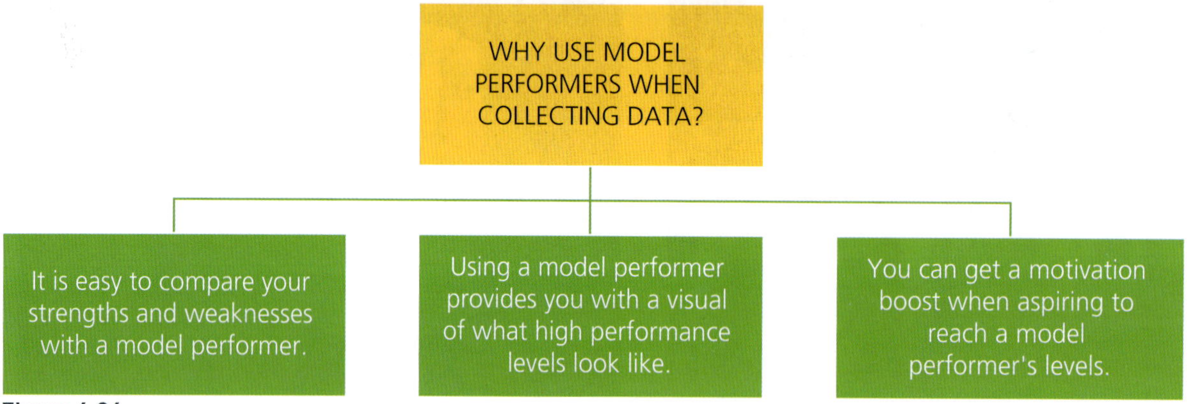

WHY USE MODEL PERFORMERS WHEN COLLECTING DATA?

- It is easy to compare your strengths and weaknesses with a model performer.
- Using a model performer provides you with a visual of what high performance levels look like.
- You can get a motivation boost when aspiring to reach a model performer's levels.

Figure 4.24

TASK 27 RECAP

1. True/False: you should use the same model performer for each of the four factors. (1)
2. Consider your response to Question 1. Justify the answer you gave. (1)
3. Identify a method of data collection for the physical factor in which a pupil compares their abilities with those of a model performer. (1)
4. What advice would you give a pupil who is struggling to structure an answer to the following question: Evaluate your performance levels in the emotional factor in comparison to a model performer. (1)
5. Explain why using an elite athlete as a model performer could be limiting. (1)
6. A pupil is considering using a classmate as a model performer when collecting data on their performance in the physical factor. Explain why they should do this. (2)

CHAPTER SUMMARY

Factor – 'Sub-factor'	Method of Data Collection
Mental: all 'sub-factors'	Performance profiling wheel (PPW)
Emotional: all 'sub-factors'	Questionnaire
Social: communication	Communication observation schedule
Physical: CRE	Bleep test
Physical: accuracy	General observation schedule (GOS)
Physical: width	Digital analysis

EXAM-STYLE QUESTIONS

1. Explain why a performer should collect data before starting a Personal Development Plan in the social factor. (2)
2. Explain reasons why a performer may wish to collect quantitative data when investigating their performance levels in the physical factor. (1)
3. Describe a qualitative method used to collect data on mental factors. (4)
4. Identify a qualitative method used to collect data on emotional factors. (1)
5. Analyse the method of data collection for the emotional factor that you identified in Question 4. (2)
6. Evaluate your strengths and areas for development in comparison to a model performer in the physical factor. (2)

TOTAL: ____/12

TIP

In your exam, use a highlighter pen to highlight the key parts of a question:

- command word
- content component: factors, data collection, developing performance, etc.
- factor
- marks available.

Doing this will help ensure you answer the question correctly and will minimise the risk of misreading it. It will also help you plan your answer in terms of content and amount of information to write. For example:

Analyse a method of data collection that can be used to gather information on the social factor. (3)

FEEDBACK

5 Feedback

The information you collect at the data gathering stage serves as feedback on your performance as it highlights your strengths and weaknesses.

FEEDBACK				
INTRINSIC: KINAESTHETIC	**INTRINSIC: THOUGHTS AND FEELINGS**	**EXTRINSIC: VERBAL**	**EXTRINSIC: WRITTEN**	**EXTRINSIC: VIDEO**
How did a skill/movement feel?	Did I get anxious, lose confidence and/or feel angry during a performance?	What did my coach and/or teammates tell me about my performance?	What do methods such as the PPW, questionnaire and/or observation schedule tell me about my performance?	What did digital analysis show me? How did my performance look compared with that of a model performer?

Figure 5.1

Feedback can be categorised into two main types:

- intrinsic feedback, which comes from within the performer
- extrinsic feedback, which comes from external sources.

Each type comes with its own specific benefits.

FEEDBACK TYPE	BENEFITS
Intrinsic: kinaesthetic	A performer receives immediate feedback on their performance, which also guides them into 'why' a skill or movement did not feel right.
Intrinsic: thoughts and feelings	Very useful for some mental and emotional 'sub-factors' where only a performer truly knows how they feel and what causes them to experience such feelings.
Extrinsic: verbal	Beneficial when received from a knowledgeable other, such as a coach who can accurately highlight elements of your performance that you are unaware of when performing.
Extrinsic: written	Serves as a permanent record that a performer can look back on to identify changes and improvements.
Extrinsic: video	Can be slowed down and paused to provide clear detail on a performance. When used with a model performer, clear comparisons can be made to help show a performer how to improve.

Table 5.1

TASK 28 INTRINSIC OR EXTRINSIC?

Match the description to the most appropriate type of feedback.

FEEDBACK TYPE	DESCRIPTION
Intrinsic: kinaesthetic	A. A footballer immediately felt down and low in self-belief when the fullback they were up against kept tackling them.
Intrinsic: thoughts/feelings	B. A dancer can see that they are out of time with the rest of their group when watching elements of their performance in slow motion.
Extrinsic: verbal	C. A golfer felt uncomfortable when performing a drive and thought that the club did not make a good connection with the ball.
Extrinsic: written	D. A basketball player sees that their lay-up is their most ineffective skill with nine tallies on the General observation schedule.
Extrinsic: video	E. A right winger in handball is continually told by their coach that they keep coming inside too much and restricting their team's width.

Regardless of the type of extrinsic feedback, it should be delivered in a manner that makes it effective.

Below is a checklist of elements that should be considered when delivering feedback.

- SOURCE: who provides the feedback? Is it the coach, who is very knowledgeable, or a teammate picked at random? This can determine how accurate and trustworthy the feedback is.
- TIMING: when is the feedback provided? Was it given immediately or several days after? This can determine how much a performer understands the information based on how much of their performance they can recall.
- ORDER: what comes first, the positives or the negatives? This can impact a performer's confidence and motivation levels, although it is important to remember that all athletes are different.
- VOLUME: how much information is provided at one time? Again, every performer is different and some can process more information than others. However, getting it right for each individual is crucial if they are to work on their performance and improve.
- INFORMATION: are strategies provided on how to improve a performance? This is often referred to as 'feed-forward' as it lets performers know what they need to do to turn a weakness into a strength.

TASK 29 USEFULNESS OF FEEDBACK

Explain how feedback received can be considered useful in the physical factor. (2)

MODEL ANSWER

Feedback on performance in the physical factor can be considered useful when information is provided on how to improve performance. This means that a performer will learn some strategies that they can use in their next training session to help turn their weakness into a strength.

> **TIP**
> Refer to the feedback considerations above when completing Task 29. Below is a model answer showing cause and effect for the 'Information' component. Use this structure to help guide your answer in two different considerations.

KEY PLANNING INFORMATION

6 Key planning information

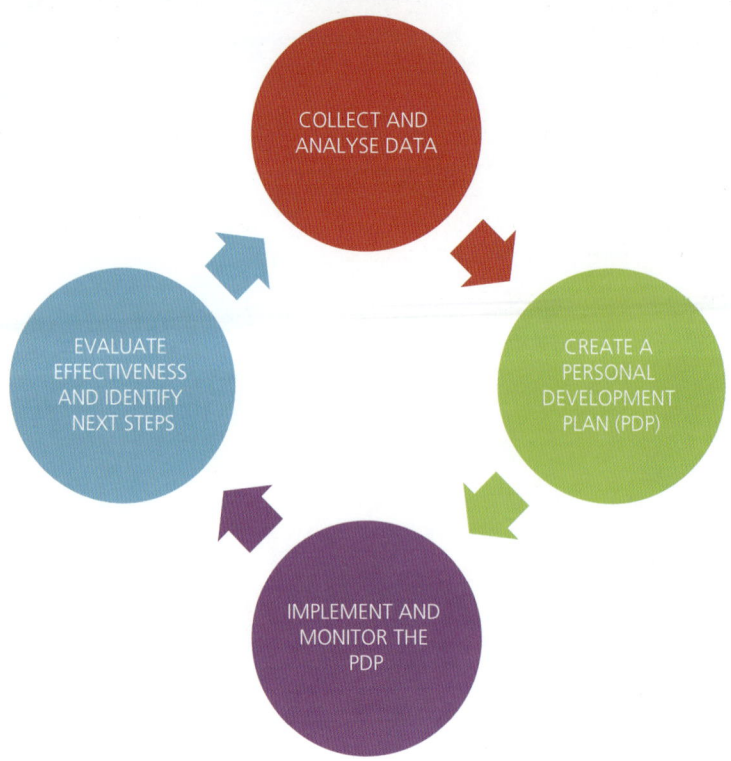

Figure 6.1

Having collected data and received feedback on your performance in each of the four factors (mental, physical, emotional and social), it is time to use this information to create a personal development plan (PDP) that improves your performance. When creating a PDP, you should consider the key planning information set out in Figure 6.2.

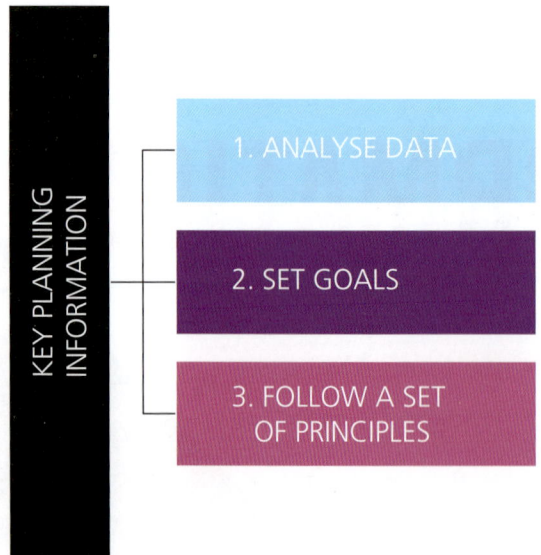

KEY PLANNING INFORMATION
1. ANALYSE DATA
2. SET GOALS
3. FOLLOW A SET OF PRINCIPLES

Figure 6.2

In considering each of these, you should be able to create an effective PDP for your identifed weaknesses. This is crucial for Section 2 of the exam, where you will be asked about PDPs you created and implemented on the Higher course.

Analysing data

The first step to planning a PDP is to analyse the results you obtained in the data collection phase. It is important that you do this because it gives your PDP a specific and appropriate focus.

TASK 30 DATA ANALYSIS

Figure 6.3 gives a summary of the results a Higher PE pupil obtained when completing the performance profiling wheel (PPW) to investigate their performance levels in the mental factor.

Identify the mental 'sub-factor' for which they should create a PDP. (1)

- CONTROLLING MY ANXIETY: 1/10
- MENTAL TOUGHNESS: 5/10
- MENTAL DATA COLLECTION RESULTS
- CONCENTRATION: 5/10
- DECISION MAKING: 6/10

Figure 6.3

> **TIP**
> 'Approach' is the title given to a training drill/activity. Do NOT confuse it with the word 'method'.

Having analysed their results and identified their biggest weakness in the mental factor, the pupil can now plan their PDP in the following ways:

- What approaches should I pick to develop my anxiety control?
- What would be a realistic long-term goal for my mental PDP?

TASK 31 PROCESS OF ELIMINATION

1. Use your problem-solving skills to delete the incorrect options in this pupil's answer. Note: there are two correct options in sentence 2 and 1 correct option in sentence 3.

   Having identified that I cannot control my anxiety levels, I have decided to create a PDP on improving this 'sub-factor'. In this PDP, I am going to include approaches such as team building games/positive self-talk/interval training/deep breathing/continuous training/role models to work on this weakness. Having scored 1 out of 10 in my baseline measurement, I am going to set a goal of 5/9 out of 10 by the end of my 3-week PDP.

2. Justify your reasoning for not selecting the other option available to you for the PDP goal. (1)

As well as helping a performer pick relevant approaches and set realistic goals, some data collection results can help plan other elements of the PDP. Consider this in regard to the bleep test.

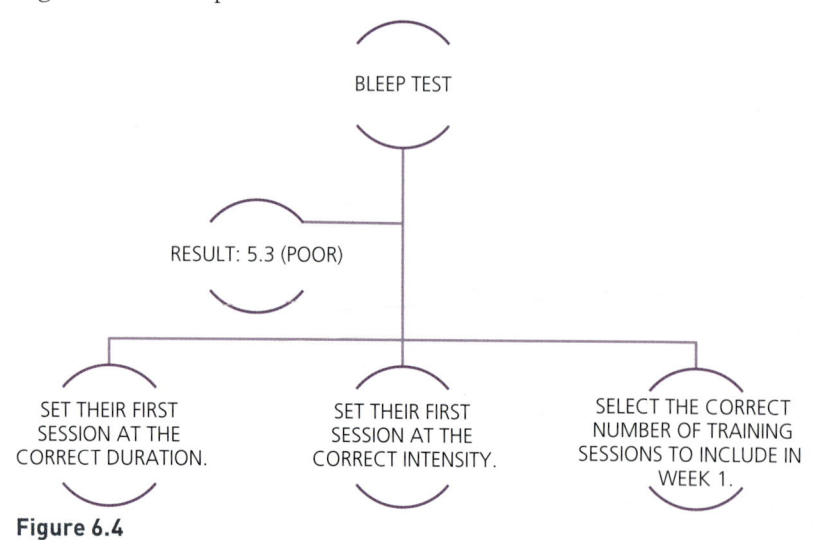

```
                        BLEEP TEST
                            |
        RESULT: 5.3 (POOR)
                            |
    ┌───────────────────────┼───────────────────────┐
  SET THEIR FIRST        SET THEIR FIRST        SELECT THE CORRECT
  SESSION AT THE         SESSION AT THE         NUMBER OF TRAINING
  CORRECT DURATION.      CORRECT INTENSITY.     SESSIONS TO INCLUDE IN
                                                WEEK 1.
```

Figure 6.4

From the bleep test result in Figure 6.4, we can see that the pupil can then use it to plan the first week of their PDP and take into account the frequency, intensity and time of their initial sessions.

Goal setting

Now that you have analysed your results, you can take this data and use it to set goals for your PDP.

```
                                    ┌─ Set for the end of your PDP.
                 ┌─ LONG-TERM GOALS ─┤
                 │                  └─ Usually based on your baseline score.
GOAL SETTING ────┤
                 │                   ┌─ Set for the end of each session.
                 └─ SHORT-TERM GOALS ─┤
                                     └─ Stepping stones on your way to achieving your long-term goal.
```

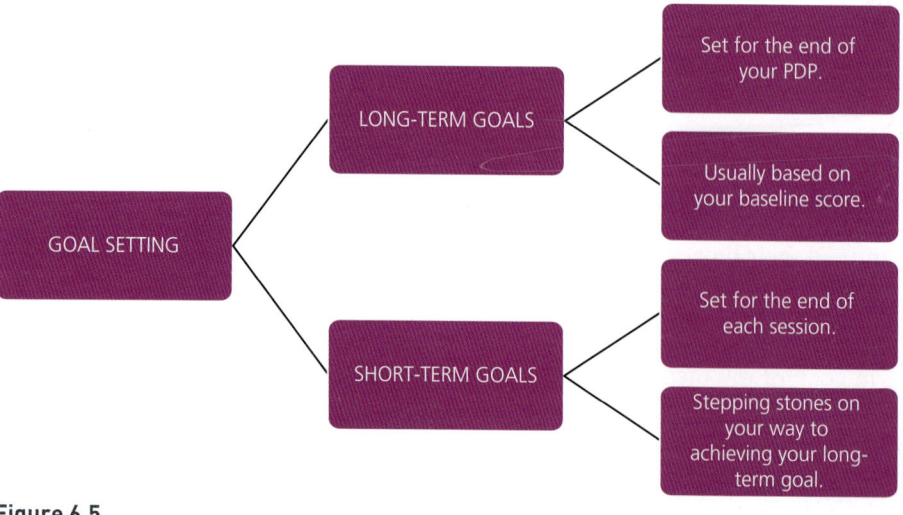

Figure 6.5

Goals can be divided into two categories:

- short-term – typically set for each session
- long-term – usually set for the end of a PDP.

Consider the short-term goals as stepping stones on the path to achieving your long-term goal.

> **TIP**
>
> In an exam, you will typically be asked to describe an example of a long-term goal and a short-term goal as a pair of questions. It is vital that you differentiate between the time given to achieve the long-term and the short-term goals.

TASK 32 GOAL SETTING

There are many reasons why we set goals before and during a PDP. Match the explain causes (1–3) to the effects (a–c).

1 Set goals to give us a motivation boost.
2 Set goals to give each session a specific focus.
3 Set goals to aid monitoring and tracking processes.
   a Encourages us to give 100% in every session to ensure that we reach our goals and improve.
   b Helps our partner, who is watching our session, by giving them a specific area to feed back on to let us know if we are on track to meet our short-term goal.
   c By checking if we are achieving each short-term goal, it lets us know if and/or how we can adapt the next session to ensure we are suitably challenged.

An acronym we can follow when setting goals is SMART (Figure 6.6). Considering each element in the SMART acronym will help us set effective goals that can successfully lead to the effects explained in Task 32.

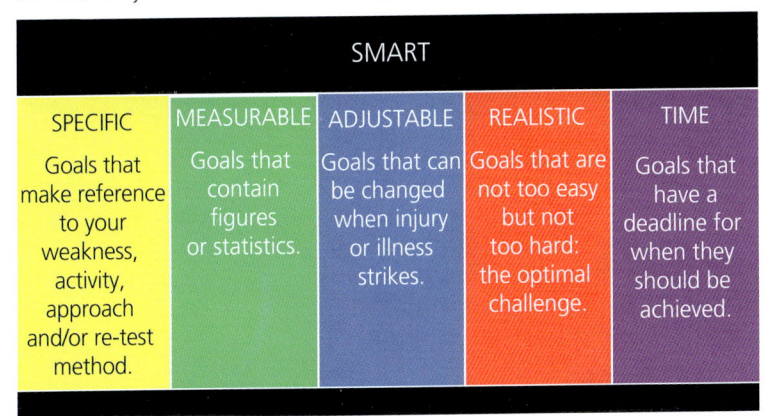

SMART				
SPECIFIC	**MEASURABLE**	**ADJUSTABLE**	**REALISTIC**	**TIME**
Goals that make reference to your weakness, activity, approach and/or re-test method.	Goals that contain figures or statistics.	Goals that can be changed when injury or illness strikes.	Goals that are not too easy but not too hard: the optimal challenge.	Goals that have a deadline for when they should be achieved.

Figure 6.6

Consider this long-term goal a pupil has set for their upcoming social PDP after they asked for passes only four times in their communication observation schedule.

By the **end of my six-week PDP**, I want to be better at **communicating by asking for a pass** at least **10 times** in my **communication observation schedule re-test in basketball**.

When we analyse this goal and deconstruct it, we can identify four of the five SMART components.

- SPECIFIC: 'sub-factor' within the game ('communicating by asking for a pass'); re-test method ('communication observation schedule') and the activity ('basketball') are stated.
- MEASURABLE: a clear figure ('10') is provided.
- REALISTIC: a realistic score ('10 times') for a six-week PDP is provided based on the baseline data.
- TIME: a clear deadline ('end of my six-week PDP') is set.

TASK 33 DECONSTRUCTION

Using the structure above as a guide, analyse the following short-term goal a Higher PE pupil has set for their emotional PDP. The pupil set this after they felt calm inside 10 deep breaths in their previous session. (4)

By the end of today's session, I want to control any anger I may feel inside 8 deep breaths.

Principles of training and principles of effective practice

There are two sets of principles that performers can follow when creating a PDP. These principles both tie into the physical factor, with one focusing on developing a performer's fitness levels and another developing their skill level. Both have elements that overlap, however, and can be used when creating a PDP for mental, emotional and social factors.

```
PRINCIPLES FOR CREATING A PDP
├── PRINCIPLES OF TRAINING
│   ├── FITNESS 'SUB-FACTORS'
│   └── SPORT
└── PRINCIPLES OF EFFECTIVE PRACTICE
    ├── SKILL 'SUB-FACTORS'
    └── VPSMARTER
```

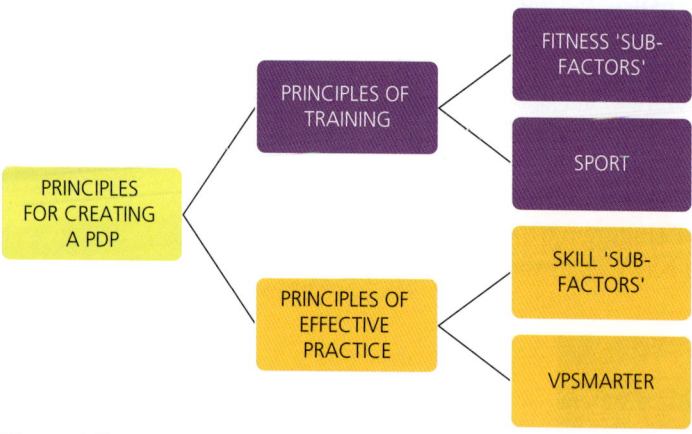

Figure 6.7

Principles of training

The principles of training provide a set of guidelines that you can follow when creating and implementing a PDP that aims to develop your physical fitness levels. An easy way to remember these principles is by following the acronym SPORT.

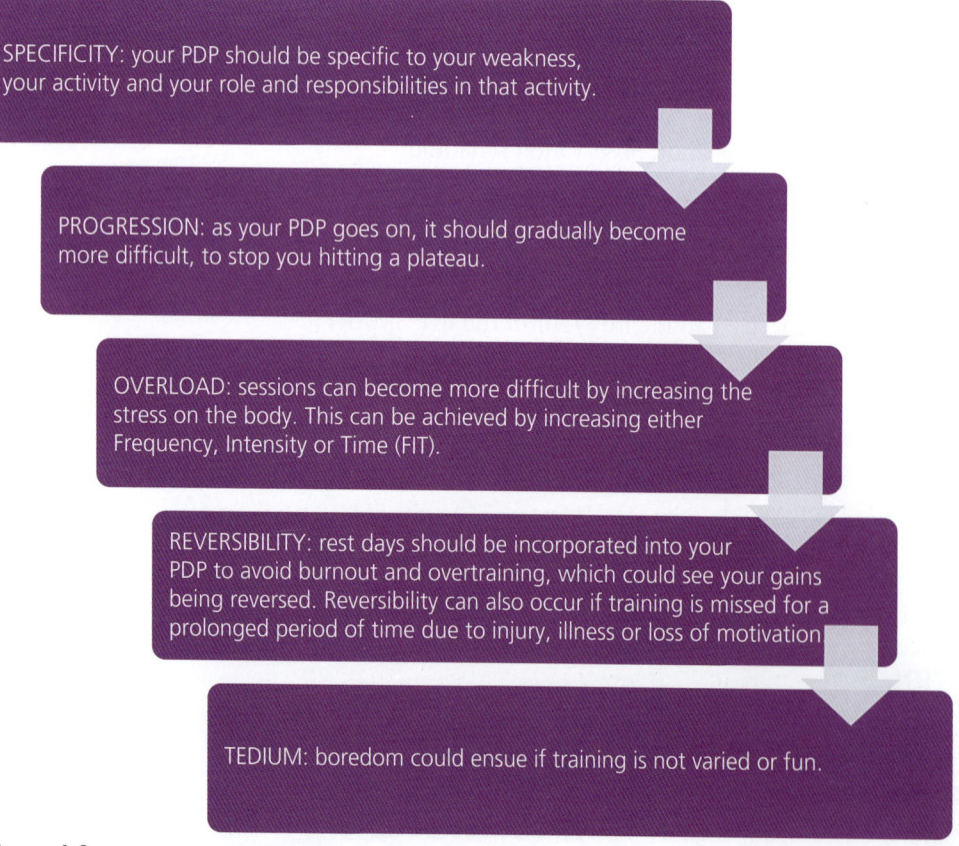

- **SPECIFICITY:** your PDP should be specific to your weakness, your activity and your role and responsibilities in that activity.
- **PROGRESSION:** as your PDP goes on, it should gradually become more difficult, to stop you hitting a plateau.
- **OVERLOAD:** sessions can become more difficult by increasing the stress on the body. This can be achieved by increasing either Frequency, Intensity or Time (FIT).
- **REVERSIBILITY:** rest days should be incorporated into your PDP to avoid burnout and overtraining, which could see your gains being reversed. Reversibility can also occur if training is missed for a prolonged period of time due to injury, illness or loss of motivation.
- **TEDIUM:** boredom could ensue if training is not varied or fun.

Figure 6.8

> **LITERACY IN PE**
>
> The term plateau means to level off or see no change. It is vital that we avoid this in a PDP.

> **TIP**
>
> We can overload…
>
> - frequency: train more often.
> - intensity: train at a higher heart rate.
> - time: train for longer in a session.

TASK 34 INCORPORATING THE PRINCIPLES OF TRAINING

Match each bullet point with the appropriate principle. Once completed, it will show you how the principles of training can actually be used when creating a PDP to develop CRE.

- A gymnast decides to use a variety of CRE approaches rather than doing the same one over and over again.
- A tennis player prefers to include interval training in their PDP as opposed to continuous training because it contains different paces, like in a match.
- A football player felt that their last two sessions were not challenging enough. As a result, they have asked their coach to make the duration of their next approach longer.
- In week 3 of their PDP, a dancer trained four days in a row and now feels exhausted. In week 4, they plan to train Monday, Wednesday, Friday and Sunday so they have a rest in between each day to minimise the risk of injury.
- A badminton player has decided to push themselves and will increase how often they train in a week from twice a week to three times a week.

PRINCIPLE OF TRAINING	EXAMPLE IN A PDP
SPECIFICITY	
PROGRESSION	
OVERLOAD	
REVERSIBILITY	
TEDIUM	

Stages of learning

Before fully switching our attention to the principles of effective practice, it is important to learn about the different stages a performer goes through when learning a skill. These stages are referred to as the stages of learning and have implications for how the principles of effective practice are implemented.

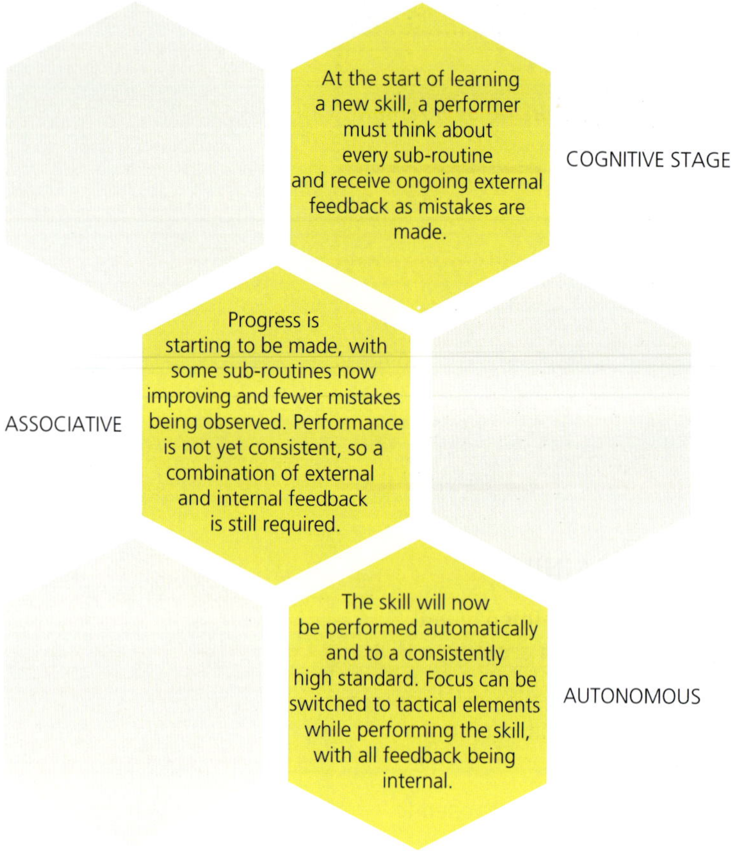

COGNITIVE STAGE
At the start of learning a new skill, a performer must think about every sub-routine and receive ongoing external feedback as mistakes are made.

ASSOCIATIVE
Progress is starting to be made, with some sub-routines now improving and fewer mistakes being observed. Performance is not yet consistent, so a combination of external and internal feedback is still required.

AUTONOMOUS
The skill will now be performed automatically and to a consistently high standard. Focus can be switched to tactical elements while performing the skill, with all feedback being internal.

Figure 6.9

> **TIP**
> A skill is broken down into different 'sub-routines'. For example, a performer doing a lay-up should take off on their opposite foot.

It is important that you are able to identify what stage you are at when learning a new skill. This is because it can aid your planning and help you create a PDP that is relevant to your ability levels.

TASK 35 STAGES OF LEARNING

As part of their homework, a Higher PE pupil was asked to write a short essay on the stages of learning and how they impacted the decisions they made when creating a PDP. Read this extract and then answer the questions that follow.

I had never performed an overhead clear in badminton before and was therefore at the cognitive stage of learning. At this stage, I decided to rely wholly on internal feedback (e.g. kinaesthetic feedback) to help me identify how the skill felt. I also decided to use an approach called a combination drill, where I had to perform the overhead clear in combination with multiple other skills during a rally.

1. In the extract, the pupil has decided to rely only on kinaesthetic feedback. Explain why this could be an issue at the cognitive stage. (1)
2. Later, they state that they used a combination drill at the cognitive stage. Explain why errors may have occurred during their training session. (1)

So, knowing your correct stage of learning can help you select relevant approaches and understand what type of feedback you should seek in order to progress your performance. The approaches and feedback types used will change as you move through each stage. See Table 6.1 for some examples of this.

STAGE OF LEARNING	APPROACH	FEEDBACK
COGNITIVE	Shadow practice: an approach that contains no pressure as movements are gradually introduced and learned without equipment.	External: an experienced and knowledgeable other such as a coach should be used here to ensure good habits are built.
ASSOCIATIVE	Repetition drill: equipment such as a shuttlecock is introduced as the targeted skill is now performed over and over again to develop muscle memory.	External: continuing to rely on an experienced other such as your coach, but it would also be useful to see the performance on video to build up your knowledge and show you where positives and negatives occur.
AUTONOMOUS	Conditioned game: the skill is incorporated within a game that tests your decision-making skills on when and where to use the skill in a game.	Internal: knowledge is now high, so a performer knows how the skill should feel, meaning they can provide accurate kinaesthetic feedback to themselves.

Table 6.1

Principles of effective practice

The principles of effective practice provide a set of guidelines you can follow when creating and implementing a PDP to develop a certain skill or technique. An easy way to remember these principles is by following the acronym VPSMARTER.

VARIETY
- A performer should use a variety of approaches to keep training interesting and to minimise the risk of boredom.

PROGRESSION
- A performer should gradually progress the difficulty of sessions by adding in opposition to or increasing the accuracy demands.

SPECIFICITY
- A performer should make their sessions specific to their stage of learning by selecting relevant approaches and utilising appropriate feedback types.

MEASURABLE
- A performer should include figures in each session's short-term goals so that success can be easily measured.

ACHIEVABLE
- A performer should set achievable short-term goals in each session to aid motivation and therefore work-rate.

REALISTIC
- A performer should make sessions as game-like as possible so that muscle memory can be developed within the context of a game.

TIME
- A performer should practise for only the correct amount of time in each session so that the movements of a skill can still be grooved without the risk of boredom setting in.

EXCITING
- A performer should add in competition to each session to make it fun and enjoyable so that they will want to attend training sessions.

RECORDED
- A performer should record their progress in each session in a training diary so they can monitor their progress and set the correct next steps for the following session.

Figure 6.10

TASK 36 PRINCIPLES OF EFFECTIVE PRACTICE

Look at the table below and match the principle of effective practice with its example.

PRINCIPLE OF EFFECTIVE PRACTICE	EXAMPLE
Variety	I made session 4 tougher than session 3 by adding in a hoop to the back of the court where I wanted the shuttle to land during my repetition drills.
Progression	After completing session 3, I discovered that my goal was far too easy, so I decided to make it harder and more realistic to my ability levels in session 4.
Specificity	I always finished each session with some sort of fun game to give me something to look forward to at the end.
Measurable	When learning the overhead clear, I decided to use a range of approaches like shadow practices, repetition drills and pressure drills to keep things interesting.
Achievable	I decided to make my repetition drill more game-like by instructing my partner to feed the shuttle to the back of the court while I was standing at the front when learning the overhead clear.
Realistic	I noted my thoughts and feelings of each session in my training diary and then used this to help me set the correct next steps.
Time	When I reached the autonomous stage, I decided to move to conditioned games so that I can learn how to make decisions about when and where to use the overhead clear in matches.
Exciting	I decided to make session 1 just 15 minutes when doing the shadow practice because I was aware that it could get boring performing without the use of a shuttle.
Recorded	In session 4, I wanted at least eight of my overhead clears to land in the targeted area.

CHAPTER SUMMARY

Figure 6.11 gives a summary of what a performer should consider when planning and then implementing a PDP.

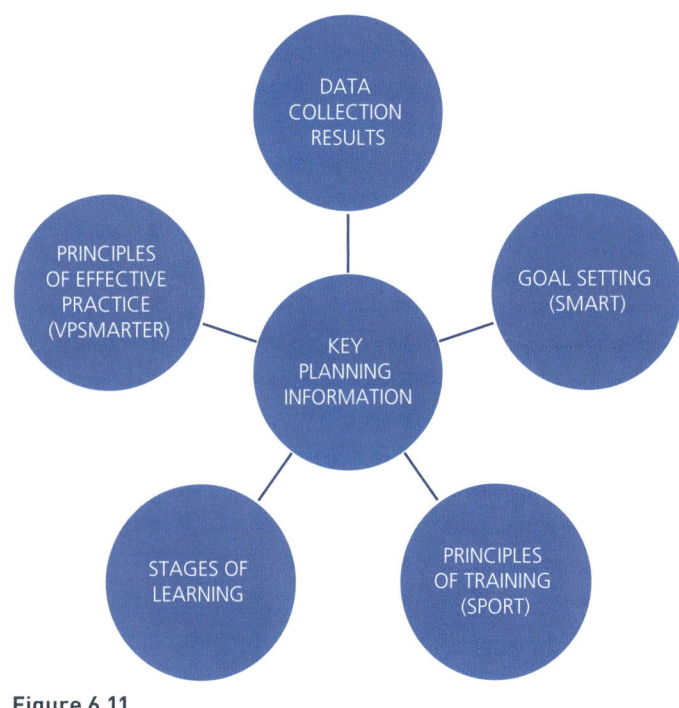

- DATA COLLECTION RESULTS
- GOAL SETTING (SMART)
- PRINCIPLES OF TRAINING (SPORT)
- STAGES OF LEARNING
- PRINCIPLES OF EFFECTIVE PRACTICE (VPSMARTER)
- KEY PLANNING INFORMATION

Figure 6.11

EXAM-STYLE QUESTIONS

1 Explain why a performer should set goals before and during a social personal development plan. (2)
2 Describe a long-term goal a performer may set for a mental personal development plan. (1)
3 Describe a short-term goal a performer may set for an emotional personal development plan. (1)
4 Analyse what a performer may consider when creating and implementing a personal development plan to develop the physical factor. (3)

TOTAL: ___/7

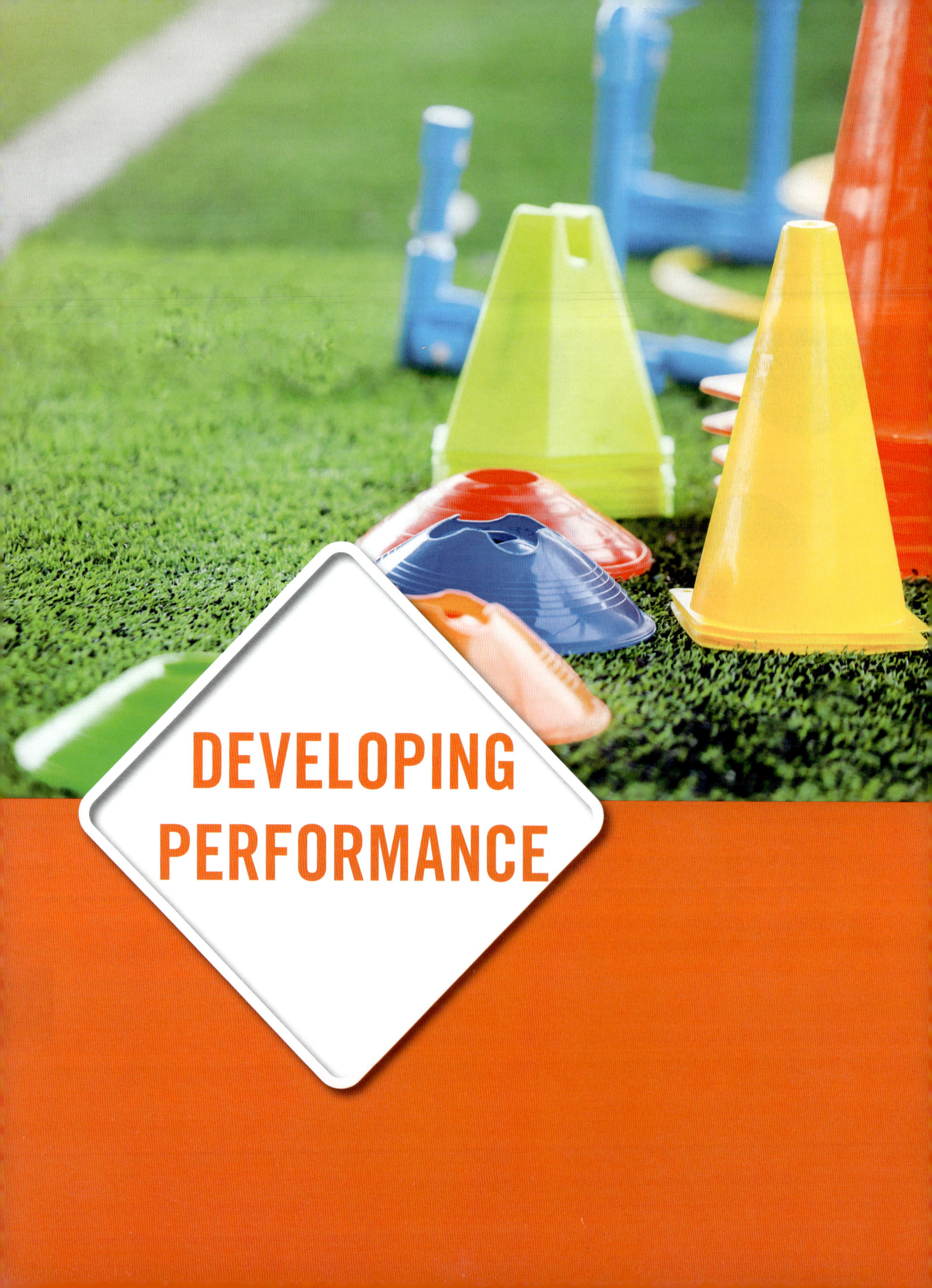

DEVELOPING PERFORMANCE

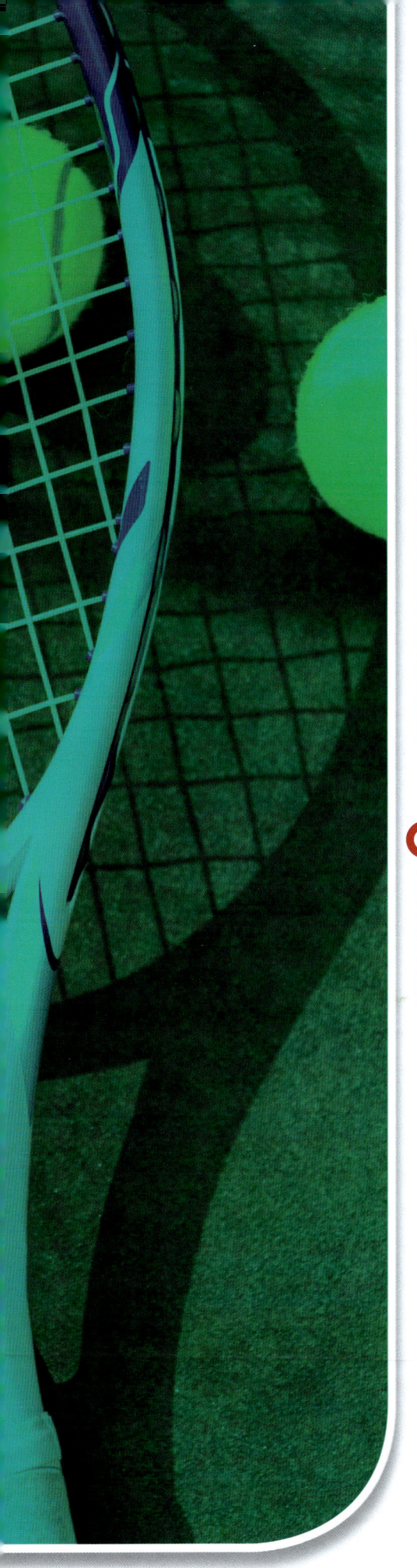

7 Developing performance

Now that you understand the processes behind creating a PDP for each factor, let's consider some of the approaches that can be included in sessions to improve your levels of performance. Table 7.1 recaps what you have covered so far for each factor, as well as the approaches you will explore in this chapter.

Factor	'Sub-factors'	Data collection method	Approaches
Mental	Anxiety Concentration Decision making	PPW	Deep breathing
Emotional	Anger Confidence Resilience	Questionnaire	Visualisation
Social	Communication Etiquette Team dynamics	Communication Observation schedule	Team-building games
Physical (fitness)	CRE	Standardised fitness test (bleep test)	Interval training
Physical (skill)	Accuracy	GOS	Shadow practice
Physical (tactics)	Width	Digital analysis	Unopposed practice

Table 7.1

> **TIP**
>
> In the Higher exam, you need to know only two approaches per factor. Make sure you learn how the command words are applied to both of your approaches. In this chapter, we will give you the information and tasks to do this for one approach per factor.

63

TASK 37 FILL IN THE BLANKS: APPROACHES

Use the word bank below to help you complete the following paragraph.

An _____ is the name given to a drill we use to develop our performance. To develop my ability in the mental factor, I will use _____. This will help me _____ and improve my _____. For the _____ factor, I will use team-building games to help develop my _____ skills and our _____. In the emotional factor, I can develop my confidence levels by _____ myself performing successfully. In the physical factor, the three different elements can be developed with specific factors; for my CRE, I will use _____; accuracy will be developed with _____ and our team's _____ in attack can be developed with _____.

> **WORD BANK**
>
> communication   interval training   focus   width
>
> deep breathing   approach   team's dynamics
>
> repetition drills   social   control my anxieties
>
> unopposed practices   visualising

Approach: mental factors
Deep breathing

> **CASE STUDY**
>
> **Sporting example**
>
> Many elite athletes use deep breathing when performing. These range from Cristiano Ronaldo to Serena Williams and the famous English rugby player Jonny Wilkinson (Figure 7.1). Wilkinson was a pioneer of using mental approaches during high-pressure situations. He credited deep breathing as an approach that helped him calm his anxieties and maintain his focus when taking conversions and penalty kicks.
>
> Figure 7.1

TASK 38 DEEP BREATHING AND COMMAND WORDS

1 Identify an approach used to develop performance in the mental factor. (1)
2 A Higher PE pupil describes below how they used deep breathing as part of their homework. However, their teacher has noticed that they have justified a number of points, which as you know is not required in a describe answer. Go through the describe answer and remove the points of justification. (3)

I initially used deep breathing at home on my own. I did this because I did not want to have teammates watching me and potentially embarrassing me for using such an approach. I also did it initially with all electronic devices turned off just to help ensure I remained fully concentrated when doing it. I breathed in through my nose for 4 seconds, then held it for 2 seconds before breathing out through my mouth for 4 seconds. This counted as 1 deep breath and I repeated this another 4 times. In my next session, I progressed the approach by reducing the number of deep breaths from 5 to 3 because I would not have long to regain my focus during a game due to its fast-paced nature.

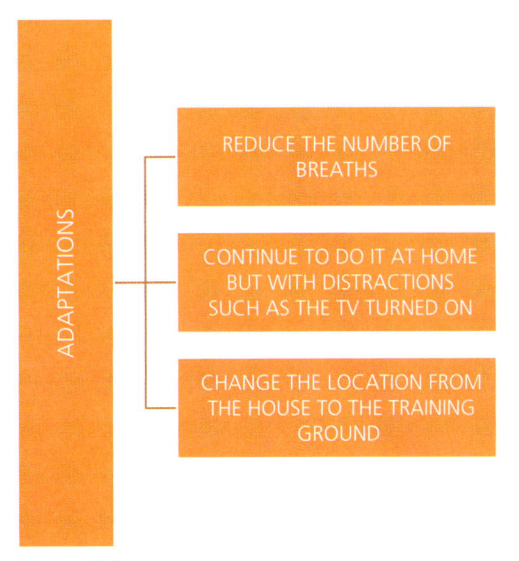

ADAPTATIONS
- REDUCE THE NUMBER OF BREATHS
- CONTINUE TO DO IT AT HOME BUT WITH DISTRACTIONS SUCH AS THE TV TURNED ON
- CHANGE THE LOCATION FROM THE HOUSE TO THE TRAINING GROUND

Figure 7.2

> **LITERACY IN PE**
>
> In the exam, you may be asked to describe and/or explain some adaptations you made during a PDP. This is simply asking you to talk through some of the changes you made. Figure 7.2 shows you some of the adaptations that could be made when using deep breathing.

There are a number of reasons why a performer may decide to use deep breathing to help develop their performance in the mental factor. Some of the causes and effects that help to explain this are shown in Figure 7.3.

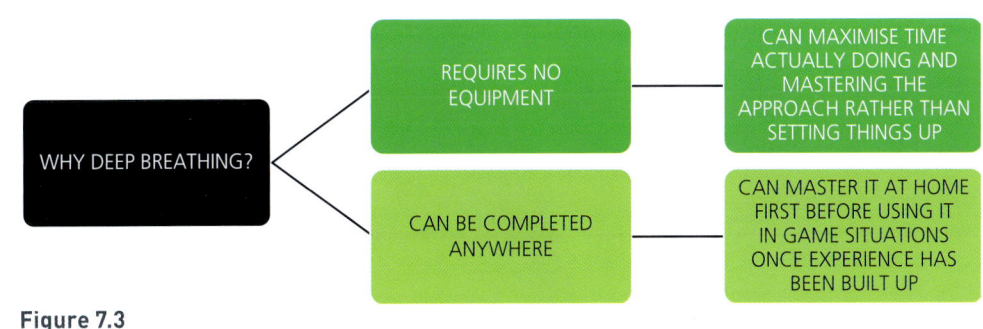

WHY DEEP BREATHING?
- REQUIRES NO EQUIPMENT → CAN MAXIMISE TIME ACTUALLY DOING AND MASTERING THE APPROACH RATHER THAN SETTING THINGS UP
- CAN BE COMPLETED ANYWHERE → CAN MASTER IT AT HOME FIRST BEFORE USING IT IN GAME SITUATIONS ONCE EXPERIENCE HAS BEEN BUILT UP

Figure 7.3

3 Can you finish off this explanation answer by providing the effect to the following cause? (Tip: consider elements such as trust.)

I used deep breathing because I have watched a number of elite athletes using it during high-pressure situations. This meant…

When evaluating an approach, an exam may ask you to either:

- evaluate the approach in regard to its benefits and limitations

OR

- evaluate how successful the approach was in developing your performance.

TIP

In the second type of question, it is vital that you provide evidence that indicates an improvement in your performance.

While some of the benefits are listed in the cause and effect diagram above, the limitations of using deep breathing can be see in Figure 7.4.

LIMITATIONS OF DEEP BREATHING	
Game situations can be very fast paced so a performer may not have the time to use it effectively in play.	Performers may feel embarrassed attempting this approach in front of their teammates.

Figure 7.4

4 Using the model answer to the right as a guide, evaluate how effective deep breathing was in helping you control your anxiety levels during a performance. (1)

TIP

It is important that you provide a broad range of evidence in your evaluation answers. Although this question has only 1 mark, in the exam it will be more and therefore it is very important that you can provide different examples to evidence the judgements you give in order to pick up maximum marks.

Consider:

Sentence 1: provide a judgement and a specific situation.

Sentence 2: provide evidence showing the impact the approach had on you.

Sentence 3: show the change in outcome it then led to in a performance.

MODEL ANSWER

Deep breathing was very effective in improving my concentration levels when serving against break point in tennis. This was effective because before serving, I was able to take a few deep breaths to help compose myself and really focus on the sub-routines I was about to perform. As a result, my concentration was better than previous matches, where I often hit a double fault as I stayed focused and hit an ace.

Having explored the benefits and limitations of deep breathing, let's now analyse some of the important aspects that make this approach work.

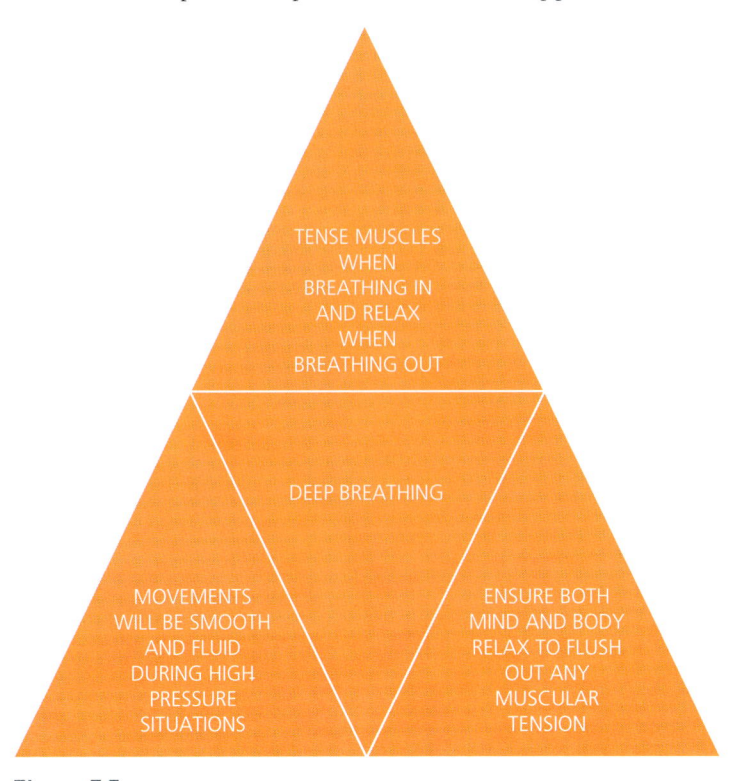

Figure 7.5

5 **a** A Higher PE pupil has said that 'it is important to gradually reduce the number of breaths as you begin to master it'. In most approaches, you would make it tougher by increasing the reps. Why do you think this pupil has suggested that deep breathing is different?
  b What impact do you think this could then have on performance?

Approach: emotional factors
Visualisation

CASE STUDY

Sporting example

A common approach that sport psychologists recommend to elite athletes is visualisation.

Before the 2012 Olympic Games, Jessica Ennis-Hill referred to the positive impact that visualisation had had in building her confidence ahead of a career-defining event.

In visualising herself as successful prior to each event in the heptathlon, she was filled with the belief that she could win gold. It also helped her to stay resilient whenever she had any bad moments during a performance because she had seen herself achieve her goals.

Figure 7.6

TASK 39 VISUALISATION AND COMMAND WORDS

1 Identify an approach used to develop performance in the emotional factor. (1)
2 Read this Higher PE pupil's answer to the question, 'Describe an approach used to develop performance in the emotional factor.' In this task, their teacher has awarded them 3/3. Go through the answer and bullet point each sentence that picks up a mark.

I used visualisation to help boost my confidence in hockey. I initially completed this approach at home on my own with all electronic devices turned off. I did this because it helped me focus on the situation I was trying to imagine. I visualised myself scoring a variety of different goals whilst including the sounds of the crowd and the sight of the opponents trying to put me off. I did this as it really helped me recreate the situation so it felt normal when I stepped on to the pitch. I repeated these images 5 times each and reduced the number of reps to 4 in my next session.

3 You have already been advised to try to achieve 1 mark per sentence when answering a describe question. This pupil has written six sentences but achieved only 3 marks. Why do you think this is? (2)

> **TIP**
>
> OPERATION: remember the board game 'Operation' when you were 'buzzed' each time you hit the metal sides? Each time you see a justification in a describe answer, imagine you receive this 'buzz' to alert you to the mistake.

Like all approaches, visualisation comes with a number of benefits and limitations. Look at Figure 7.7, then answer task questions 4 and 5.

BENEFITS
- Requires no equipment
- Used by elite athletes
- Can be completed anywhere

LIMITATIONS
- Can it be used in fast-paced game situations?

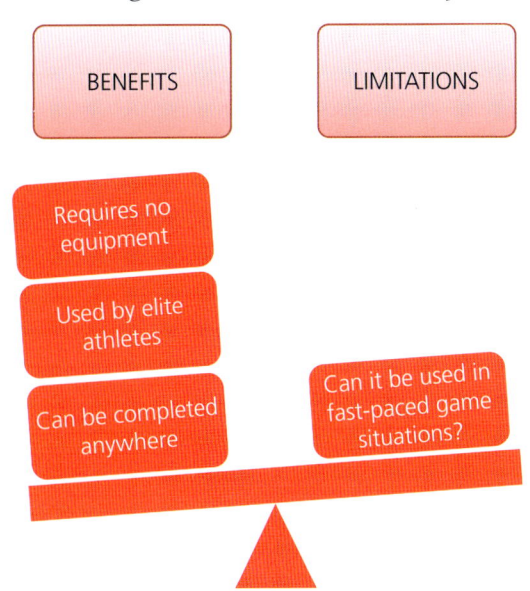

Figure 7.7

> 4 Look at Figure 7.7 and match the correct benefits with the effects below in order to build a 2/2 explanation answer.
> - This meant that I fully trusted the usefulness of the approach and gave it my all in order to master it and use it effectively.
> - This meant that I wasted no time setting things up and I was able to focus on mastering the approach.

In the mental approaches section, we evaluated deep breathing in relation to the impact it had on your performance. In this section, we will instead switch our attention to simply evaluating the benefits and limitations of visualisation.

> 5 A Higher PE pupil has judged visualisation to be 'slightly effective'. Evaluate the benefit that is different from those you explained in Question 4, then evaluate the limitation given in order to finish off this pupil's answer. (2)
>
> *Visualisation was slightly effective in boosting my confidence in the emotional factor.*

Let's consider some of the different aspects that makes visualisation work. Remember, as part of any analysis, we will follow a certain structure:

a Deconstruct: if we were to break visualisation apart into small areas, what areas must be there to make this approach work?
b Why: provide a reason why we have identified this part as being important to the process of completion.
c Impact: what impact does this then have on developing performance?

Figure 7.8

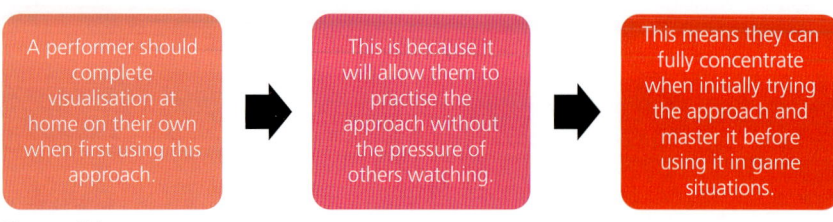

- A performer should gradually decrease their number of reps to progress visualisation.
- This is because they will ultimately want to use Visualisation during breaks in play during a performance.
- This means they will be able to see themselves being successful in one take, which will give them a quick confidence boost during moments when time is short.

Figure 7.9

- A performer should complete visualisation at home on their own when first using this approach.
- This is because it will allow them to practise the approach without the pressure of others watching.
- This means they can fully concentrate when initially trying the approach and master it before using it in game situations.

6 MIND THE GAP: fill in the 'why' part of this three-step analyse answer.

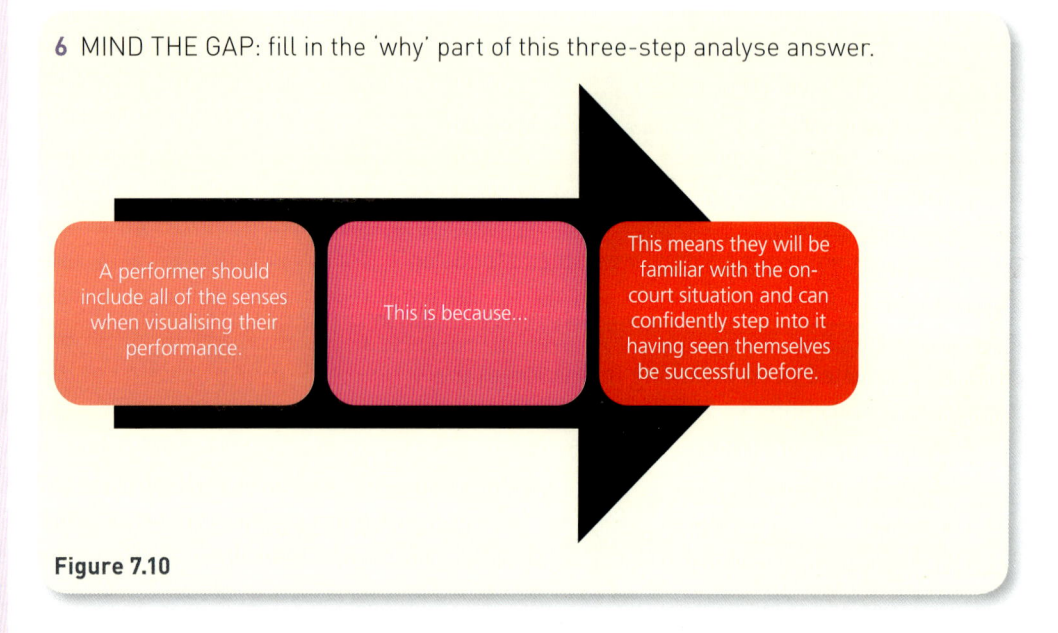

- A performer should include all of the senses when visualising their performance.
- This is because…
- This means they will be familiar with the on-court situation and can confidently step into it having seen themselves be successful before.

Figure 7.10

Approach: social factors

Team-building games

Team-building games are often used in sport and business to bring teams together. A variety of team-building games can be used to help **develop individuals' communication skills and relationships with others**. Three examples of team-building games include:

- human knot
- blindfold obstacle course
- birthday line-up game.

TEAM-BUILDING GAMES		
HUMAN KNOT	BLINDFOLD OBSTACLE COURSE	BIRTHDAY LINE-UP GAME

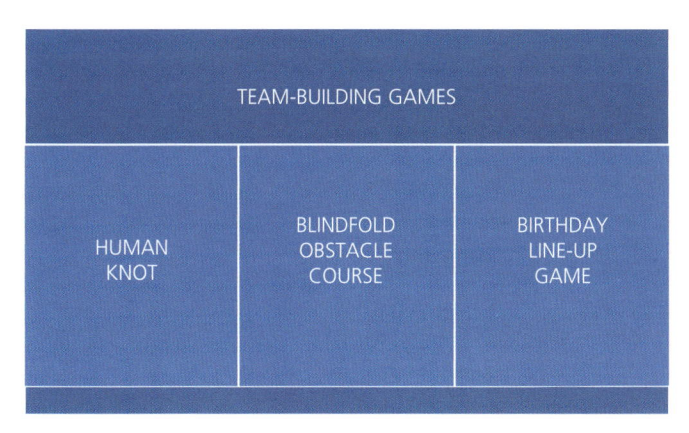

Figure 7.11

TASK 40 TEAM-BUILDING GAMES AND COMMAND WORDS

Figure 7.12

In this section, we will specifically focus on the human knot.

1 Identify an approach used to develop performance in the social factor. (1)
2 Read the description below, then answer the questions that follow.

The human knot involves getting into a group of 8 and forming a circle. Each individual places a hand into the middle and grabs the hand of someone not standing next to them. They then place their other hand in and repeat this but grab somebody different. On the teacher's whistle, they then try to untangle themselves without breaking links. Should a link be broken, they must separate and start the process again. The approach is over once the group have fully untangled themselves and are standing in a clear circle. The human knot can be progressed by increasing the number of participants to 10 in the next session.

    a How many participants take part in the human knot?
    b True/False: a performer grabs the hand of the person next to them.
    c What happens if two people in the group break links?
    d At what point is the human knot over?
    e Describe a progression that could be made to the human knot.

3. Table 7.2 gives a number of reasons why a performer may choose to use team-building games. Match up the causes and effects to access the full 3 marks to the following question:

   Explain reasons why a performer may use a certain approach to develop performance in the social factor. (3)

Cause	Effect
I chose the human knot because it required no equipment.	This meant we became familiar with voicing our opinions and issuing instructions, which we were then able to take on to the pitch.
I chose the human knot because it forced us to communicate to solve the problem of untangling the knot.	This meant we enjoyed working together and our team dynamics grew as we looked forward to taking part in these sessions.
I chose the human knot because it was fun.	This meant we were able to get into the approach quickly and work on developing our team dynamics rather than wasting time setting things up.

Table 7.2

We will now switch our attention to evaluating the effect this approach has on performance levels. Remember, in this question we are not concerned with the benefits and limitations of team-building games but rather with the changes they bring about in performance. As discussed, it is very important to show a breadth of knowledge here in order to give a number of different examples that will allow you to pick up marks.

In Figure 7.13, we show you how communication can be improved in a variety of ways by team-building games.

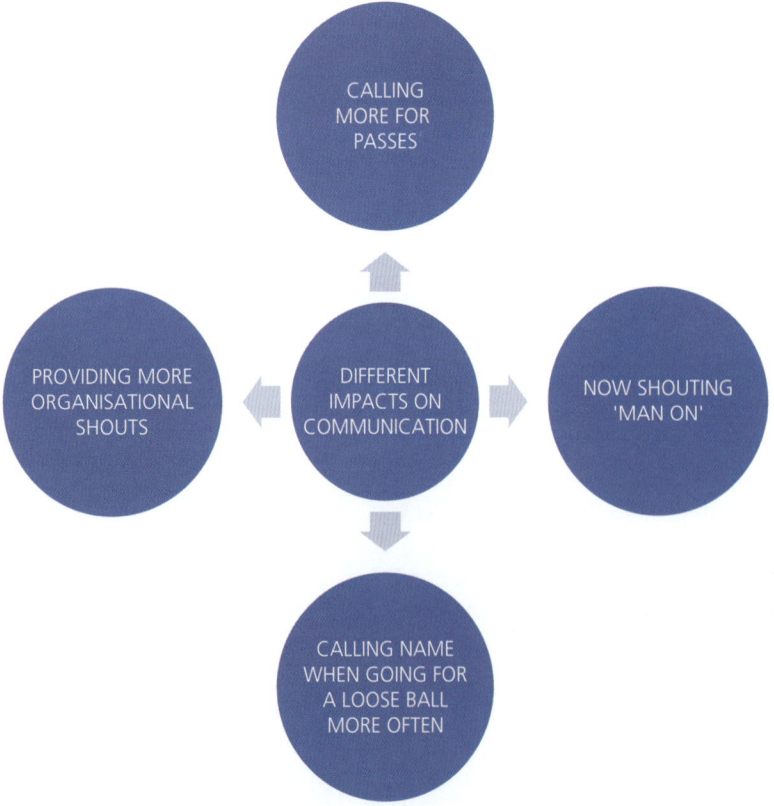

Figure 7.13

Centre: DIFFERENT IMPACTS ON COMMUNICATION
- CALLING MORE FOR PASSES
- NOW SHOUTING 'MAN ON'
- CALLING NAME WHEN GOING FOR A LOOSE BALL MORE OFTEN
- PROVIDING MORE ORGANISATIONAL SHOUTS

TIP

Show your breadth of knowledge by using the same 'sub-factor' a number of times across different situations and/or by using different 'sub-factors' within a factor.

4 Using the model answer below as a guide, evaluate one other way in which team-building games brought about an improvement in a performer's communication skills. (1)

MODEL ANSWER

Team-building games really improved my communication skills during a rally in volleyball. My ability to talk improved when the ball came over the net and was about to land between my teammate and I as I called loudly to alert them to the fact I would play the shot. This resulted in them moving out the way and giving me space to play an accurate dig, whereas before I would not have communicated, and confusion would have occurred.

> **TIP**
>
> NOTICE how during this evaluative answer there is a clear judgement demonstrating the change and where it occurred in an activity. From there, evidence is given showing what this change did to the performer. Finally, the impact on performance is noted, with the change further highlighted in comparison with what would have happened before.

5 Figure 7.14 shows different components of an analyse answer. Number them to create two coherent analyse answers. (2)

- It is important that you complete team-building games with a variety of different teammates.
- This means you will be able to collaborate on court to overcome any problems that arise during a performance.
- This is because it will allow you to communicate and build relationships with everyone in your team.
- This is because it will force your team to communicate and work together in order to achieve the task.
- It is important that any team-building game contains a problem that needs to be solved.
- This means that you will be able to work with, and support, all of your teammates on court regardless of your position or whether subs have been made.

Figure 7.14

Approach: physical factors (fitness)

Interval training

As mentioned in Chapter 6, when planning a PDP, a performer should consider the activity they participate in if they are to choose approaches that are appropriate to their development. The vast majority of activities performers participate in require a change of pace. It is for this reason that interval training is often chosen as an approach to develop an athlete's CRE levels.

Figure 7.15

TASK 41 INTERVAL TRAINING AND COMMAND WORDS

1 Identify an approach used to develop performance in the physical factor. (1)
2 A netball player has just completed an interval training session in week 1 of her CRE PDP. She has written the following description:

I completed a 20-minute interval training session around the outside of my team's netball court. In this, I worked at a 50:50 ratio of slow jogging for 20 seconds and going at a ¾ pace for 20 seconds. Throughout this time, I tried to stay between 70-85% of my maximum heart rate (HR). I completed this session with a partner who had similar CRE levels to me.

Based on their description of their session details and the fact that they found the session easy, can you give them two different options to progress the difficulty of this session next time out? (2)

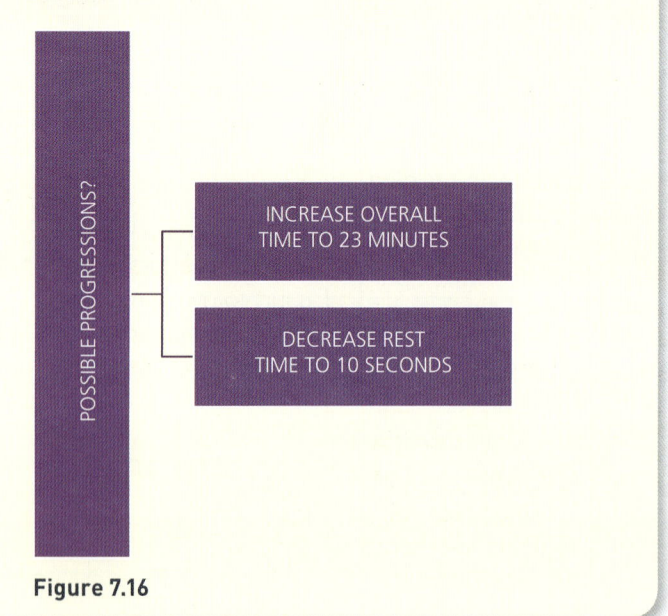

POSSIBLE PROGRESSIONS?
- INCREASE OVERALL TIME TO 23 MINUTES
- DECREASE REST TIME TO 10 SECONDS

Figure 7.16

TIP

When describing an approach, you do NOT get marks for describing how it is set up. You do, however, pick up marks for stating a way in which it was progressed.

As with other explanation answers, it is vital that your causes and effects fit together if you are to be awarded marks. Remember to always ask yourself 'SO WHAT?' after you have written your cause to push you towards writing the correct effect in sentence 2.

> **3** Below is a pupil's answer that explains why they selected interval training as an approach to develop their CRE levels. In their answer, they scored only 1/3. Your task is to:
> **a** Identify the paragraph that obtains a mark. (1)
> **b** Correct the paragraphs that did not pick up marks. (2)
>
> I chose interval training to develop my CRE levels because it was easy to progress the duration of my sessions. This meant that I wasted little time setting things up and I was able to maximise time training and developing my CRE.
>
> I also chose interval training to develop my CRE levels because it was specific to my activity, netball. This meant that the constant changing of pace mirrored what happens in a netball match and I developed my CRE in a way that it helped me fulfil my specific role and responsibilities.
>
> Finally, I chose interval training to develop my CRE levels because it required very little equipment. This meant that I was able to work in my HR training zones for longer and develop my CRE levels without hitting a plateau.

While the answers can be considered to be some of the benefits of interval training, there are also some limitations to this approach. For the first time, we will introduce you to a different type of explain question before moving on to evaluate.

In Question 4, the structure of using cause and effect remains, although you need to explain the negative now rather than the reason why you selected interval training.

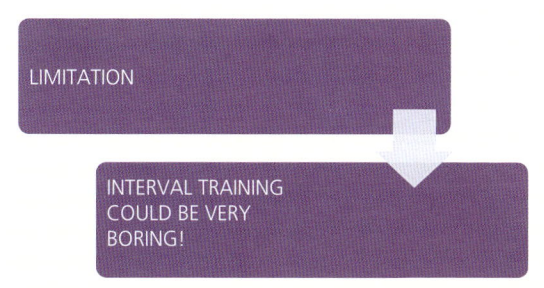

> **4** Explain why an approach you have used to develop performance in the physical factor could be limited. (2)
> **5** Using the answer below to guide you, can you explain the limitation in Figure 7.17? (1)
>
> Interval training could be limited because a very large part of it is performed at extremely high intensity levels. This means that the injury risk is higher for performers, which could stop them finishing a session and mean being out of action for several weeks.
>
> LIMITATION → INTERVAL TRAINING COULD BE VERY BORING!
>
> **Figure 7.17**

> **TIP**
>
> It is impossible to predict the exam questions you will face. Sometimes, the examiners will place the command word against course content in a novel way. It is therefore important that you use your problem-solving skills to work your way around such issues.

6 GUESS THE QUESTION: having explored two of the different types of evaluate questions you may face when evaluating approaches, read the two answers in Figure 7.18 and write down the correct questions they are answering.

GUESS THE QUESTION		
A. Interval training was very effective because it was easy to increase the intensity. This was effective because all I had to do was reduce my rest time between sprints to make the session tougher. This resulted in me working harder throughout my session and improving.	What are the correct evaluate questions?	B. Interval training improved my ability to man-mark my opponent in basketball. This was because I had developed my CRE whilst going at different paces so when my opponent tried to accelerate away from me in the final quarter, I was able to accelerate too and keep up with them. As a result, I was able to mark them out of the game, whereas before I would have been too tired and they would have got away from me.

Figure 7.18

7 A performer is analysing whether or not to work with a training partner who has the same CRE levels as them in their upcoming interval training session. Help analyse this for them and give them advice on what they should do. To strengthen your argument, remember to follow the three steps to analyse:
- Deconstruct: what should they do?
- Why: give them a reason to support your choice.
- Impact: finish off by providing the effect it could have on their training performance.

> **TIP**
>
> When analysing an approach, some pupils find it easier to pretend they are advising someone. Doing this helps them deconstruct the approach before strengthening their argument with the why and the impact.

Approach: physical factors (skill)

Shadow practice

Figure 7.19

Shadow practice is an approach that is used by performers who are in the cognitive stage of learning. At this time, they are just starting to learn about a skill and how to perform it. It is vital that they are able to practise without pressure while receiving accurate feedback from a highly knowledgeable person such as their coach. For these reasons, the shadow practice is ideal for learners at this early stage.

TASK 42 SHADOW PRACTICE AND COMMAND WORDS

1 Identify an approach used to develop performance in the physical factor. (1)
2 Below is a list of descriptive bullet points. Not all of them relate to the shadow practice. Your job is to pick out the ones that build up a describe answer for this approach, then write them out in an ordered paragraph. (4)
   - This approach was progressed by increasing the number of repetitions to 12 in each of the 3 sets.
   - We got into a group of 8 and formed a circle.
   - I aimed to play the shuttle into the hoop at the back of the court.
   - I pretended to perform a smash over and over again while using no equipment.
   - During this approach, I received double the points every time I won the rally with a smash.
   - I completed this approach for 3 sets of 10 repetitions during my session.
   - I looked to change pace from a slow jog to a ¾ pace every 30 seconds.
   - During the drill, my partner and I had to play a combination of high serve, overhead clear and drop shot before we could play for points.
   - After each attempt, I received feedback from my coach on the way I performed different sub-routines.
   - My partner would put me under pressure by playing a shot to a different part of the court as I was in the middle of executing my previous shot.

There are numerous benefits to using the shadow practice, which can explain reasons why a performer may opt to use this approach when developing their skilled performance.

3 Figure 7.20 shows a range of causes and effects a performer may consider when explaining why they use the shadow practice. Go through the figure and match each cause and effect to obtain 3 explanation marks. (3)

TIP
Ensure that you are always challenged so you do not hit a plateau.

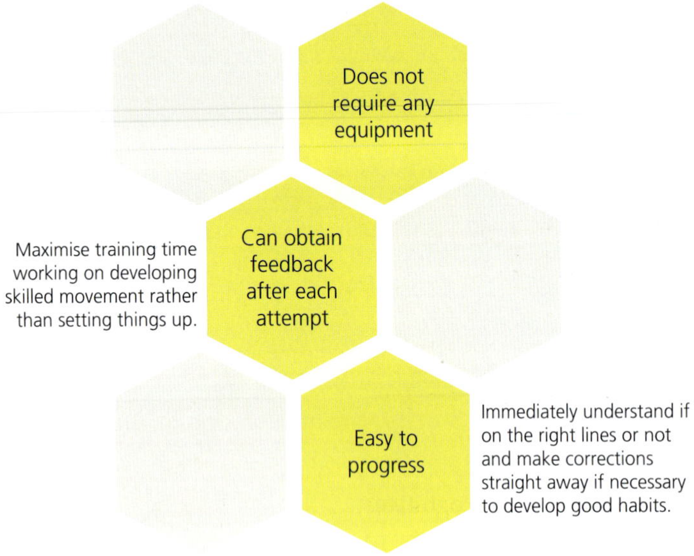

Hexagons:
- Does not require any equipment
- Can obtain feedback after each attempt
- Easy to progress
- Maximise training time working on developing skilled movement rather than setting things up.
- Immediately understand if on the right lines or not and make corrections straight away if necessary to develop good habits.

Figure 7.20

4 However, a major limitation of the shadow practice is its tedious nature. A Higher PE pupil has recognised this as part of their evaluation. Look at the paragraph below and pick out the phrase that…
   a highlights the initial judgement in sentence 1. (1)
   b provides the evidence for this in sentence 2. (1)
   c gives the effect of this on performance development in sentence 3. (1)

The shadow practice started to become ineffective due to how tedious it was. This was ineffective because as the session went on and I made my way into my 3rd set, I did start to get bored at not being able to hit the shuttle and measure my progress in performing my skill development. This resulted in me losing motivation in the final set and I did not train as well as I could have done.

TIP
After providing a judgement in sentence 1 and the evidence in sentence 2, always finish with the effect it then had on your evaluation. This shows a level of higher-order thinking skills as you understand the further impact an approach has on your training performance.

TIP
When analysing, it is sometimes useful to consider some of the limitations of an approach. The important deconstruction part could then become a solution to the problem as this will improve the process of using the approach.

Let's now analyse the shadow practice and look at some of the aspects that can make this approach work.

Look at some of the points of analysis below before completing Question 5.

[Arrow flowchart:]

- You should set a specific goal during shadow practice sessions.
- This is because it will give your partner a clear sub-routine to look out for and feed back on.
- This means it will help you develop one sub-routine at a time which suits your cognitive stage of learning.

[Second flowchart:]

- You should select a knowledgeable partner to provide you with feedback during the shadow practice.
- This is because they will understand how a skill should look and give you appropriate feedback.
- This means they will help you correct any weaknesses and you will develop the correct muscle memory.

Figure 7.21

5 Figure 7.21 gives a possible solution to the tedious nature of the shadow practice. Fill in Figure 7.22 by giving the reason why this part has been identified and then the impact it would have on your performance in training. (2)

- You should add in game-related movements prior to the shadowed skill movements in each rep.
- This is because...
- This means...

Figure 7.22

Approach: physical factors (tactics)

Unopposed practice

Unopposed practice is used when learning a new strategy or tactic. It involves walking through a set play without any opposition in order to help build familiarity with the strategy your coach is trying to develop.

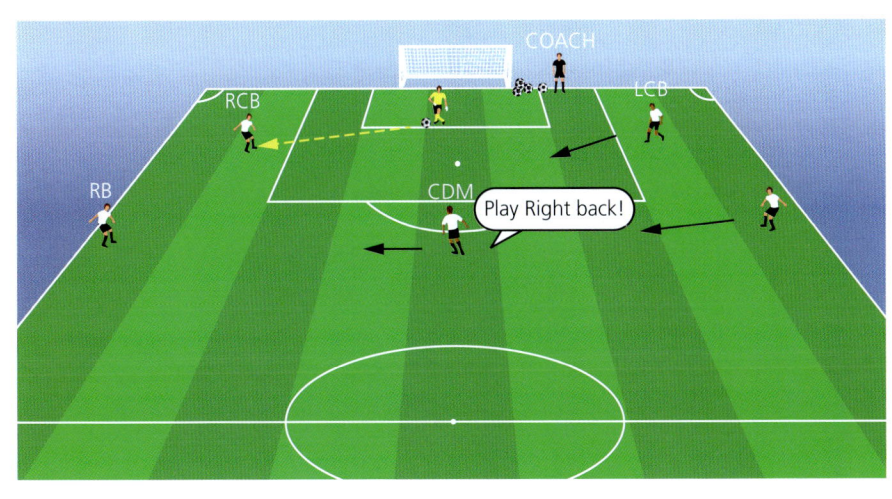

Figure 7.23

TASK 43 UNOPPOSED PRACTICE AND COMMAND WORDS

1 Identify an approach used to develop performance in the physical factor. (1)
2 Compare and contrast: below are two Higher PE pupils' descriptions of an Unopposed practice. Read them both, then answer the questions that follow.

Pupil A: We used the unopposed practice to develop our team's ability to play out from the back in football. In this, we got into our positions on the pitch and walked through how we wanted to move the ball from the goalkeeper to the striker. We did this without any pressure because we wanted to master our movements before trying it out in a game. Throughout this, the coach would stop the play when they saw something they did not like and give us instructions on how to improve it.

Pupil B: We used the unopposed practice to improve how we played out from defence in football. This was effective because it allowed us to learn our movements and the options open to us when we were in these situations in games. Throughout the approach, our coach gave us a combination of video and verbal feedback by showing us what we did well and how we needed to improve. This was useful because we were able to see our strengths and weaknesses.

    a How many marks would you give each descriptive response? (2)
    b Identify a good descriptive point in both Pupil A's and Pupil B's responses. (2)
    c Identify one sentence in each response that did not get a mark and give a reason why each identified sentence did not get a descriptive mark. (2)

3 A football coach wants to develop their team's ability to use the width of the park when attacking in football. They are unsure which approach to use to develop this aspect of their team's play. Using Figure 7.24 to help you, can you explain to them why they should consider using the unopposed practice? (2)

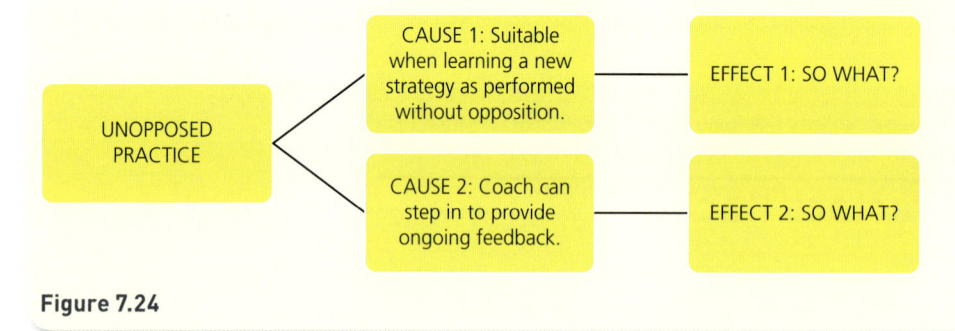

```
                    ┌──────────────────────┐      ┌──────────────────┐
                    │ CAUSE 1: Suitable    │      │                  │
                    │ when learning a new  │──────│ EFFECT 1: SO WHAT?│
                    │ strategy as performed│      │                  │
┌──────────────┐   │ without opposition.  │      └──────────────────┘
│  UNOPPOSED   │───┤                      │
│  PRACTICE    │   ├──────────────────────┤      ┌──────────────────┐
└──────────────┘   │ CAUSE 2: Coach can   │      │                  │
                    │ step in to provide   │──────│ EFFECT 2: SO WHAT?│
                    │ ongoing feedback.    │      │                  │
                    └──────────────────────┘      └──────────────────┘
```

Figure 7.24

TIP

When evaluating an approach, ensure that you do not contradict yourself. Your benefit(s) and limitation(s) should still fit together. In this task, it is important that you do NOT pick a benefit and a limitation that contradict each other.

4 As well as the benefits, the unopposed practice is limited, as Figure 7.25 illustrates. Use Figure 7.25 to pick one benefit from above and one limitation from below and write an evaluation answer that follows the judgement of 'slightly effective'. (2)

LIMITATION 1

BORING WITHOUT ANY OPPOSITION

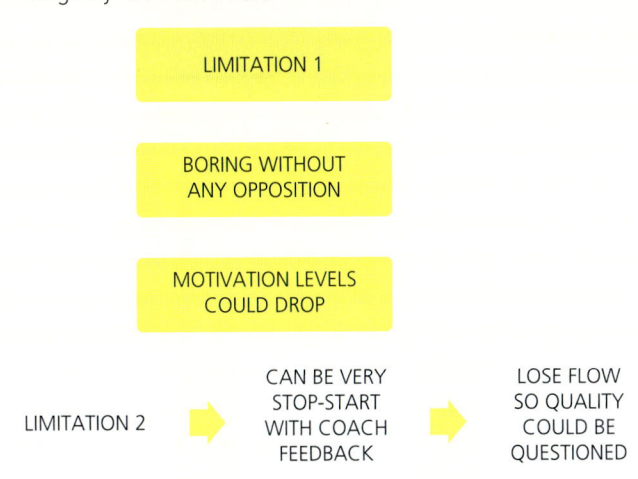

MOTIVATION LEVELS COULD DROP

LIMITATION 2 → CAN BE VERY STOP-START WITH COACH FEEDBACK → LOSE FLOW SO QUALITY COULD BE QUESTIONED

Figure 7.25

5 a Having been persuaded to use an unopposed practice in their upcoming session, the coach is now looking for advice on how to use the approach correctly. Ideally, they would like two things to consider when using the approach. Table 7.3 shows three parts to an analyse answer (deconstruct – why – impact). Number them to create two analyse answers that help advise the coach on how to use Unopposed practices correctly. (2)

DECONSTRUCT	WHY	IMPACT
The coach should provide ongoing feedback throughout the Unopposed practice.	This is because it will make the practice more exciting and make the performers more motivated when completing the approach.	This means good habits can be formed as mistakes are eradicated and the players will be suitably prepared to try this strategy with some opposition.
The coach could add in a points system upon completing each repetition of the unopposed practice.	This is because your players are still learning how to implement the strategy and will ultimately make mistakes.	This means they will be more focused during the session and try harder in order to achieve more points, which ultimately sees them train better.

Table 7.3

b Looking at the two points of analysis you have created, which one overcomes the limitation of tedium identified in the evaluation section of the unopposed practice? (1)

7 Developing performance

CHAPTER SUMMARY

Table 7.4 lists the approaches we have covered in this chapter.

Factor	Approach
Mental	Deep breathing
Emotional	Visualisation
Social	Team-building games
Physical (fitness)	Interval training
Physical (skills)	Shadow practice
Physical (tactics)	Unopposed practice

Table 7.4

Having completed our guided discovery tasks, why not test your knowledge with the following exam-style questions. Before doing so, remember some of the tips provided in this chapter:

- When describing an approach you used, you will NOT get marks for saying how it looked. This applies only to methods of data collection and NOT approaches.
- When evaluating your approaches, read the question carefully. If the evaluate question refers to 'improving/developing performance', then your answer must show changes in a performance as opposed to the benefits and limitations of the approach.

With this in mind, attempt the questions below and compare your answers with those in the marking guide at the back of the book.

EXAM-STYLE QUESTIONS

1 Describe an approach used to develop performance in the social factor. (4)
2 Explain why you used a certain approach to develop your performance in the emotional factor. (2)
3 Analyse an approach a performer may use to improve performance in the physical factor. (2)
4 Consider an approach used to develop performance in the physical factor.
   a Evaluate the effectiveness of this approach. (2)
   b Evaluate how effective this approach was in developing your performance. (2)

TOTAL: ___/12

FACTORS IMPACTING PERFORMANCE DEVELOPMENT

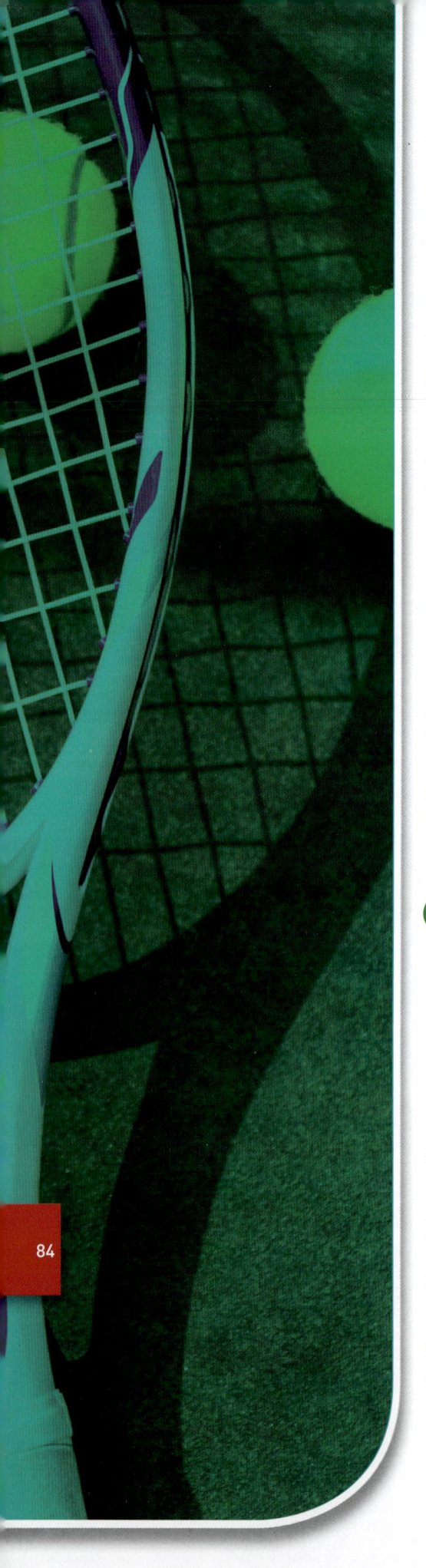

8 Factors impacting performance development

Factors do not only impact your performance during an activity, they can also impact your performance during training. Consider this question from the 2019 Higher PE exam:

Explain the impact any improvements in social factors can have on the performance development process. (2)

This question type has become more prominent in recent exams. However, pupils often answer poorly, simply referring to factors impacting performance. The key is in analysing (deconstructing) the question and identifying the phrase 'performance development'. When answering such questions, we slightly adapt the three-step factors impacting performance structure to a new three-step structure highlighted in Figure 8.1.

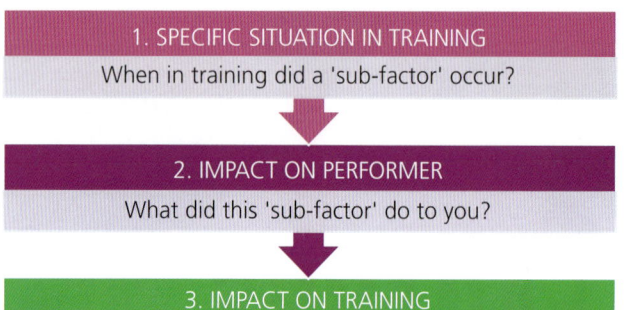

1. SPECIFIC SITUATION IN TRAINING
When in training did a 'sub-factor' occur?

⬇

2. IMPACT ON PERFORMER
What did this 'sub-factor' do to you?

⬇

3. IMPACT ON TRAINING
What then happened in the training situation as a result?

Figure 8.1

> **EXAMPLE**
>
> Explain how mental factors could impact performance development. (1)
> Mental toughness helped me in the final sprint set of my interval training session. This meant that despite feeling tired, I battled through the pain to give one final burst. This resulted in me sprinting as fast as I could in this final set to help develop my CRE levels.

Why is this a good answer?

1 Specific training situation provided: 'final sprint set'.
2 Buzz words used to demonstrate understanding of mental toughness: 'battled through'.
3 Clear outcome linked to training stated: 'sprinting as fast as I could'; 'develop my CRE'.

Chapter 4 will show you how two different 'sub-factors' from each factor can impact the performance development process.

Mental factors

Concentration

Performers need to focus during every single training session. This will enable them to concentrate on key instructions and feedback from their coach as well as to really focus on their progress towards each session's short-term goal (Figure 8.2).

```
CONCENTRATION ─┬─ FOCUS WHEN LEARNING A NEW SKILL IN A SHADOW PRACTICE
               └─ FOCUS ON THEIR IMAGE WHEN USING VISUALISATION
```

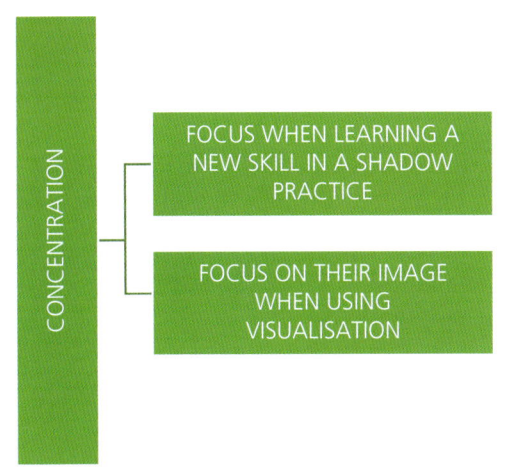

Figure 8.2

EXAMPLE

Being able to concentrate helped me when using visualisation with the TV on for the first time. This meant that I was able to focus on recreating the match situation in my head whilst blocking out the sounds from the TV. This resulted in me producing a clear image and I boosted my confidence as I consistently saw myself score.

TIPS

Just because the question may ask you to consider the impact of mental factors on performance development does NOT mean the training situations should also be in a mental PDP.

Be creative and consider ANY training situation where a 'sub-factor' may occur. It opens up the door to many more marks.

TASK 44 CONCENTRATION

Using the example answer above, can you use the three-step process in training to help build upon the training situation in Figure 8.3? (1)

```
[I had to concentrate when learning a new skill in the shadow practice.] → [This meant...] → [This resulted in...]
```

Figure 8.3

Motivation

Motivation is how much desire a performer has to achieve their training goals. The more a performer wants to achieve success, the harder they will work in training sessions to reach their goals.

Note: being highly motivated does not solely mean that a performer will work hard during their PDP; it could also lead to them doing extra outside of their programme to help them reach their goals quicker. Look at the example of footballer Cristiano Ronaldo (see case study) to see how being motivated led to him doing extra.

CASE STUDY

Sporting example

In 2006, Cristiano Ronaldo wanted to fulfil his potential and become one of the best football players in the world. Motivated by this goal, he went to the gym to develop his strength and stayed behind after training for extra shooting practice. As a result, he became stronger, which helped him fend off the tackles of defenders as well as improve his free kick and penalty-taking abilities to boost his goalscoring record in 2007.

Figure 8.4

TASK 45 BE THE EXAMINER: MOTIVATION

A Higher PE pupil has written an answer explaining how motivation impacted their performance when trying to develop their CRE levels. Go through their answer and give them feedback using the questions below.

A lack of motivation stopped me training at my best level halfway through an interval training session. This meant that I started to get bored and no longer wanted to continue due to the lack of a skill element in the session. This resulted in me not working as hard as I could during the sprinting sets and my CRE did not improve as well as it could have done.

a   Why is sentence 1 a very good start to this pupil's answer? (1)
b   Identify buzz words in sentence 2 that show that the pupil understands how motivation could impact them. (1)
c   How is this pupil's sentence 3 better than that of their classmate's, who wrote the following in sentence 3: 'This resulted in my CRE not improving'? (1)

Emotional factors

Anger

A number of things can occur during a session that can make a performer angry (Figure 8.5). In many cases, this can lead to poor performance in training; however, in some cases it could actually stimulate a performer to work harder and to improve.

Figure 8.5

> **TASK 46 ANGER**
>
> Using these example answers to help you, analyse how a performer getting angry at making mistakes during a repetition drill can negatively impact their training performance. (1)
>
> I got angry when my teammates were messing around during the human knot. This meant that I got frustrated at them not taking the task seriously and started shouting and criticising them. This resulted in arguments breaking out and, rather than working together, our team dynamics actually dropped.
>
> I channelled my anger after being criticised by my coach during a conditioned game. This meant that I controlled my anger and channelled it into trying to prove them wrong in the game. This resulted in me working even harder and winning the next rally with a drop shot to win double points.

Resilience

The whole point of training is to turn a weakness into a strength. This learning process is a non-linear one, meaning that you will make mistakes as you attempt to reach your training goals (Figure 8.6). It is therefore vital that you are resilient in these moments and learn from them in order to keep developing and moving forward.

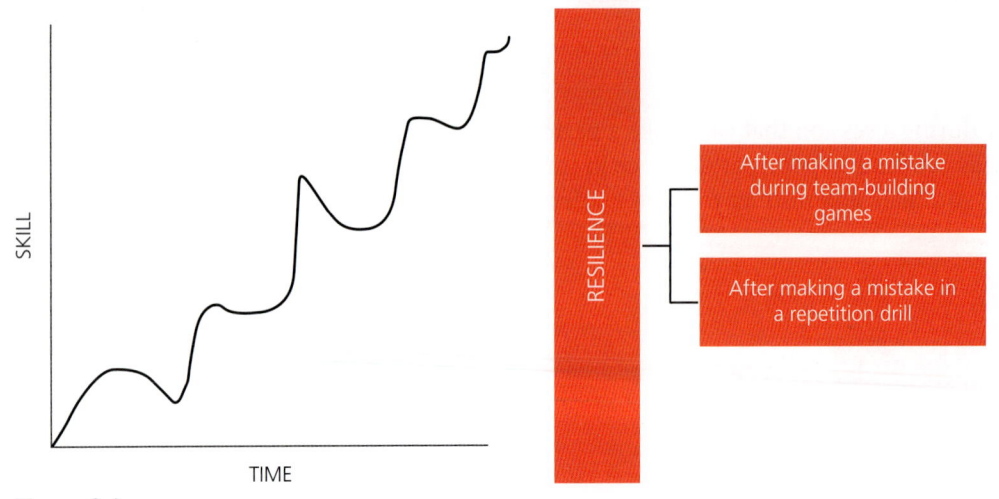

Figure 8.6

TASK 47 RESILIENCE

The training situations in Figure 8.5 are outlined in Table 8.1 with the rest of their potential answers. Piece together the correct three-step process for each to produce two different answers showing the impact that resilience can have on the performance development process. (2)

SPECIFIC SITUATION	IMPACT ON PERFORMER	IMPACT ON TRAINING
Being resilient helped my team after we made the wrong move in the human knot.	This meant that I bounced back by seeking feedback from my coach on why I missed rather than dwelling on it.	This resulted in me really focusing on my footwork on the approach to the basket and being more accurate in my next attempt.
Having high levels of resilience helped me after I missed a lay-up in a repetition drill.	This meant that we bounced back from the error by reflecting on why it went wrong and explored different moves.	As a result, we stuck together and made the correct next move, which helped us move forward in fully untangling ourselves.

Table 8.1

Social factors

Communication

Being able to talk as well as listen will always help you perform well in training. Communicating is vital, whether that be in terms of providing and/or receiving feedback or contributing your ideas to the group when learning a new tactic. Figure 8.7 gives two more specific examples of when communication could aid the performance development process.

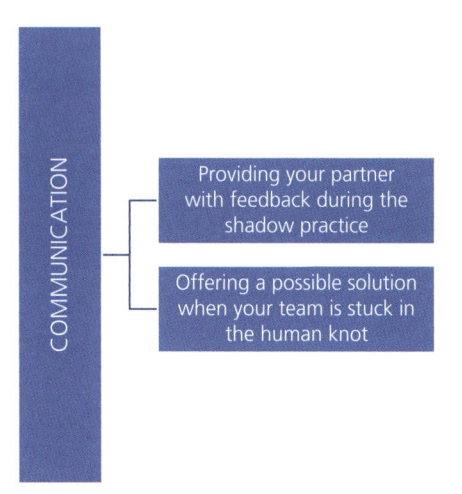

```
COMMUNICATION ─┬─ Providing your partner
               │   with feedback during the
               │   shadow practice
               │
               └─ Offering a possible solution
                   when your team is stuck in
                   the human knot
```

Figure 8.7

Consider this pupil's answer on the impact that communication had on their performance when trying to learn how to shoot in netball.

My partner's communication really helped me learn the different sub-routines of shooting in netball when doing a shadow practice. This meant that they were able to clearly tell me what I was doing wrong and, crucially, give me clear information on how to improve. This resulted in me taking on board their feedback and correcting the error to better develop my muscle memory.

In this answer, the pupil does very well because they:

- clearly state when in the shadow practice the communication helped them – this enables them to be specific
- use buzz words like 'clearly' to show how their partner was effective in feeding back to them
- end with a clear outcome showing how they improved their performance as they corrected 'the error to better develop my muscle memory'. Again, specific.

TASK 48 COMMUNICATION

Using this as a guide, can you take the other example in Figure 8.7 through the three-step process?

Co-operation

Co-operation is the ability to work together in order to achieve a desired outcome. In some cases, one team member may demonstrate a selflessness by going out of their way to help a teammate improve (Figure 8.8).

```
          ┌─────────────┐
          │ An injured  │
          │  teammate   │
          │  providing  │
          │ advice during│
          │ an Unopposed│
          │   Practice  │
          └─────────────┘
                 │
          ┌─────────────┐
          │     CO-     │
          │  OPERATION  │
          └─────────────┘
           /           \
┌──────────┐           ┌──────────────┐
│ Spotting │           │  A teammate  │
│   your   │           │ staying behind│
│ teammate │           │ to provide feeds│
│ during a │           │ to you when  │
│ weights  │           │ you are doing│
│ session  │           │ extra practice│
└──────────┘           └──────────────┘
```

Figure 8.8

TASK 49 FILL IN THE BLANKS: CO-OPERATION

Use the word bank below to help you fill in the blanks.

My co-operation skills enabled me to _____ my partner when they were doing extra practice on their drop shot in badminton. This meant I _____ to stay behind with them and _____ to the back of the court. This resulted in their extra practice _____ due to my feeds, and they developed their drop shot.

My partner showed excellent co-operation skills when I was struggling to bench press in a weights training session. This meant that they _____ me by spotting my reps and _____ when I was tiring to push the bar up. This resulted in me feeling more _____ to push through the pain and less _____ of hurting myself as I knew they were there to help me improve my strength.

WORD BANK

assisted   gave up my time   fearful   support

giving me encouragement   being more game-like

motivated   provide them with feeds

Physical factors

Accuracy

Being accurate in your skill execution is important for both yourself and your teammates during a host of different practices. In this section, we will look at what would happen if you were inaccurate and how this could negatively impact the performance development process (Figure 8.9).

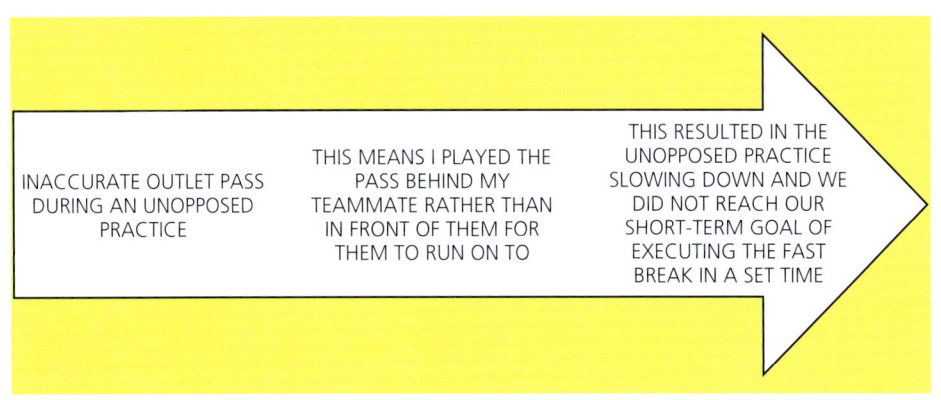

| INACCURATE OUTLET PASS DURING AN UNOPPOSED PRACTICE | THIS MEANS I PLAYED THE PASS BEHIND MY TEAMMATE RATHER THAN IN FRONT OF THEM FOR THEM TO RUN ON TO | THIS RESULTED IN THE UNOPPOSED PRACTICE SLOWING DOWN AND WE DID NOT REACH OUR SHORT-TERM GOAL OF EXECUTING THE FAST BREAK IN A SET TIME |

Figure 8.9

TASK 50 ACCURACY

Use Figure 8.9 to help you complete Figure 8.10. Try to consider how your inaccuracies could impede your partner's development and what these inaccuracies prevent them from building up.

> **TIP**
>
> Similarly to factors impacting performance, if you are providing a positive and a negative answer, you must show a breadth of knowledge with different situations to avoid 'flipping' your answer (i.e. contradicting yourself).

This resulted in...

This meant...

My lack of accuracy hindered my partner's development when they were trying to improve their smash in a repetition drill.

Figure 8.10

Muscular endurance

Muscular endurance is the ability of a set muscle group to perform the same action over and over again without tiring. Similarly to other 'sub-factors', this can impact both your own and your teammates' performance in training. In this section, we will show you how to write a positive and a negative answer without contradicting yourself.

> **TIP**
> One way to avoid repetition or contradiction in these questions is to change the focus from your performance development to you helping your partner's performance development in different situations.

MUSCULAR ENDURANCE
- ARMS AND SHOULDERS STAYING FRESH IN THE FINAL SET OF A REPETITION DRILL
- LEG MUSCLES TIRING WHEN SHOOTING DURING A PRESSURE DRILL

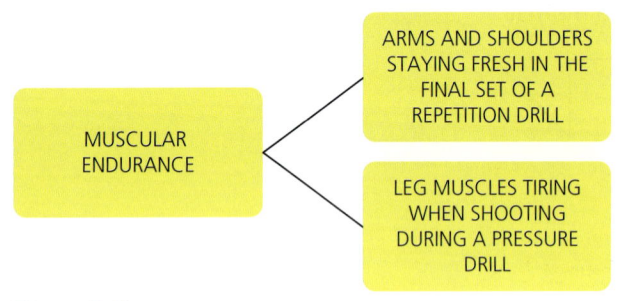

Figure 8.11

TASK 51 SPOT THE DIFFERENCE

Read both answers below, then answer the questions to help your comparing and contrasting abilities.

Answer A
High levels of muscular endurance in my arms and shoulders helped me in the final set of a repetition drill to develop my overhead clear. This meant that my arms and shoulders remained fresh in what was ultimately my 30–36th repetitions of the session. This resulted in me being able to continue practising my sub-routines in each rep to maximise my improvement.

Answer B
However, low levels of muscular endurance in my legs did not help my teammates' performance in goals during a pressure drill. This meant that during the final set, my legs were too tired when shooting and I did not put our goalkeeper under enough pressure. As a result, they were not as tested as well as they could have been and their reflexes did not improve as intended.

a Look at sentence 1 in each answer. Identify the 'when' in each to make both answers specific. (2)
b In sentence 2 of both answers, what are the buzz words that demonstrate that this pupil understands the impact that muscular endurance had on them? (2)
c What is the difference in outcomes of sentence 3 in both answers? (1)

CHAPTER SUMMARY

In the Higher exam, you can be asked about factors impacting performance development. This is different from factors impacting performance as you must refer to the impact of factors on training. Figure 8.12 gives some tips we covered in this chapter.

TIPS

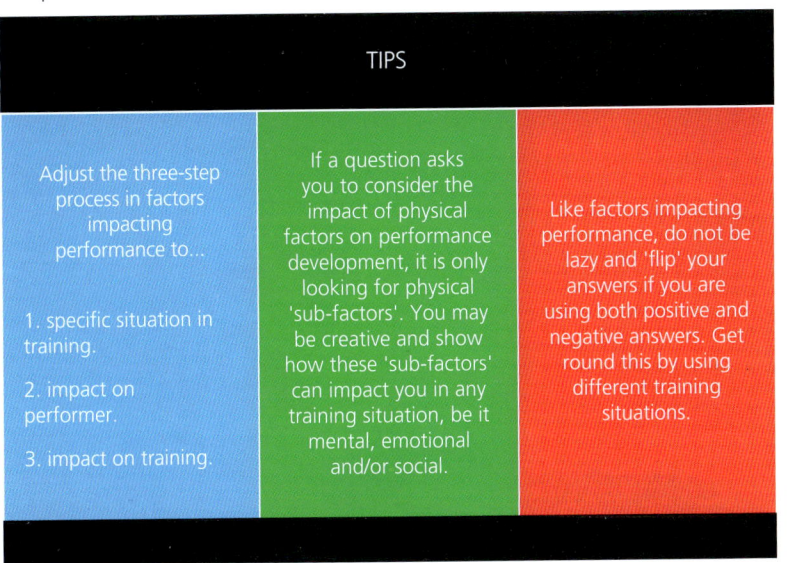

| Adjust the three-step process in factors impacting performance to… 1. specific situation in training. 2. impact on performer. 3. impact on training. | If a question asks you to consider the impact of physical factors on performance development, it is only looking for physical 'sub-factors'. You may be creative and show how these 'sub-factors' can impact you in any training situation, be it mental, emotional and/or social. | Like factors impacting performance, do not be lazy and 'flip' your answers if you are using both positive and negative answers. Get round this by using different training situations. |

Figure 8.12

EXAM-STYLE QUESTIONS

1. Analyse the impact that mental factors could have on performance development. (1)
2. Explain how reductions in emotional factors could impact the performance development process. (1)
3. Explain how social factors could impact performance development. (1)
4. Analyse how improvements in the physical factor could impact the performance development process. (1)

TOTAL: ___/4

TIP

Where it says 'reductions', you must respond with a negative answer and where it says 'improvements', you should give a positive answer. If neither is stated, you can go either way with your answer.

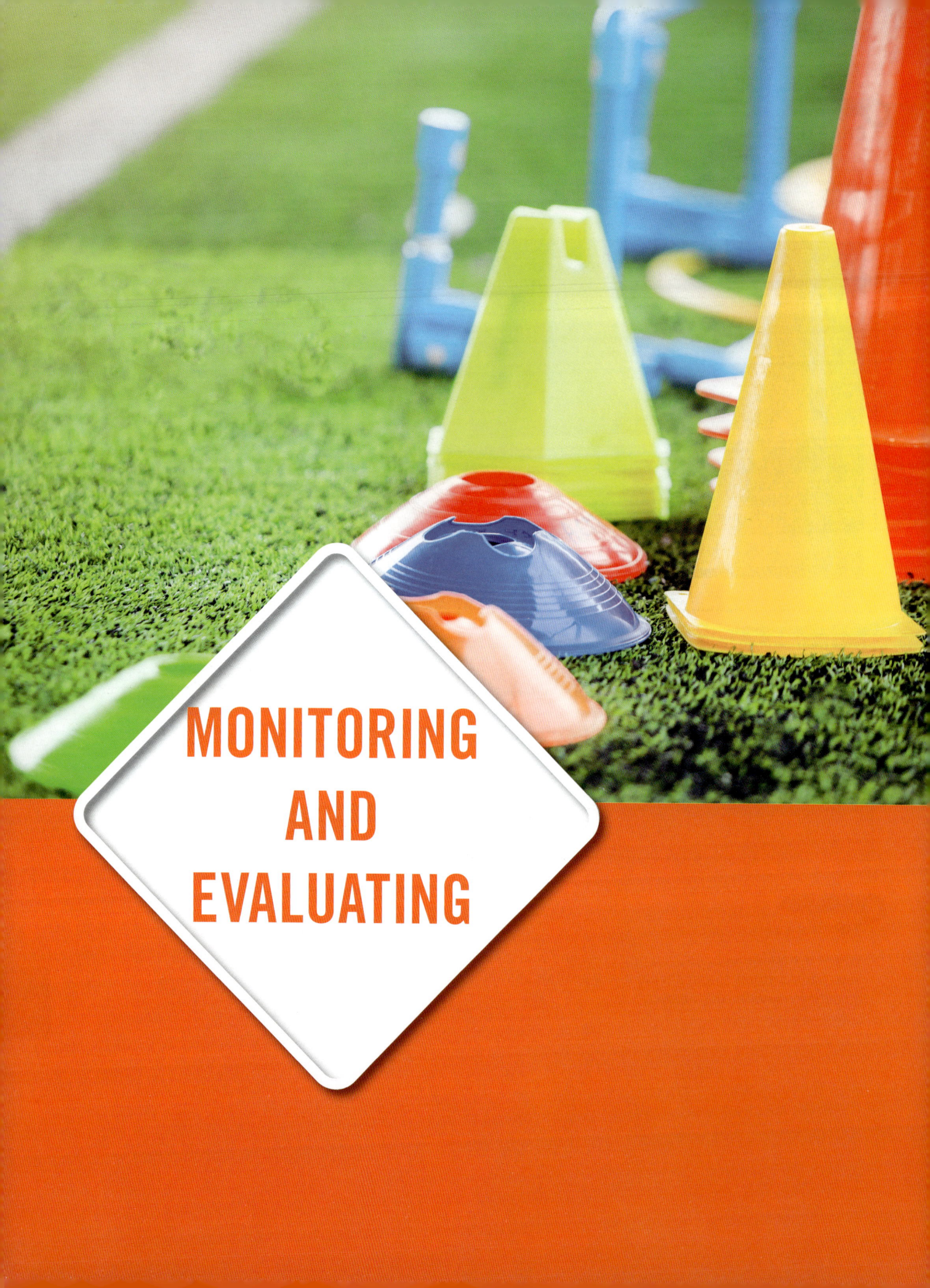

MONITORING AND EVALUATING

9 Monitoring and evaluating

As we near the end of the cycle of analysis, we engage in two new processes: monitoring and evaluating.

Reviewing your progress in your PDP as you work your way through it.

MONITORING

EVALUATING

Looking back at the end of your PDP to judge how effective it was in developing your performance.

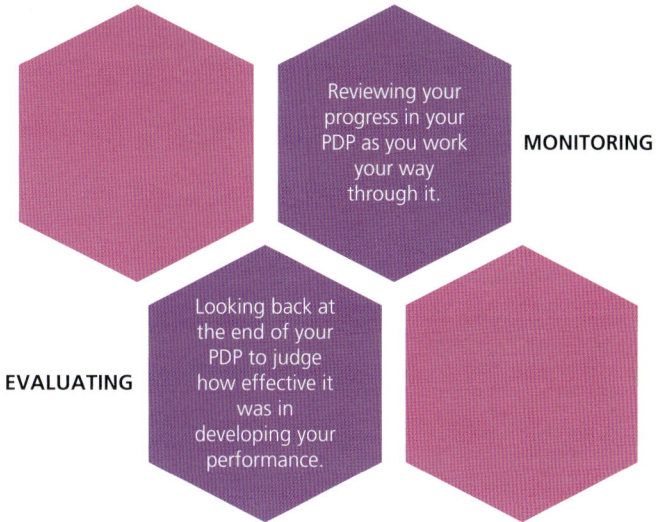

Figure 9.1

It is vital that you understand the differences between monitoring and evaluating.

TASK 52 FILL IN THE BLANKS

Use the word bank to help you fill in the blanks and develop your understanding of the differences between monitoring and evaluation.

Monitoring occurs _____ a PDP whereas evaluating occurs at the ____ of the PDP.

Monitoring involves you looking back after _____ to see how it went: what were the _____ of the session? From here, _____ can be made to ensure the PDP continues to provide you with an appropriate challenge.

Evaluating involves _____ how effective the PDP was in developing your performance. It helps you answer questions such as: Did I reach my _____? Do I have any new _____ that I can take back through the cycle of analysis? Doing all of this will help you make a suitable judgement on the effectiveness of your PDP.

WORD BANK

each session	judging	during
adaptations	development areas	end
positives and negatives	long-term goal	

There are many reasons why a performer should both monitor and evaluate their progress during and after a PDP. Look at Figure 9.2, which gives numerous causes and effects that would help you answer the following question:

Explain why a performer should monitor and evaluate their progress in the _____ factor. (4)

WHY MONITOR AND EVALUATE?

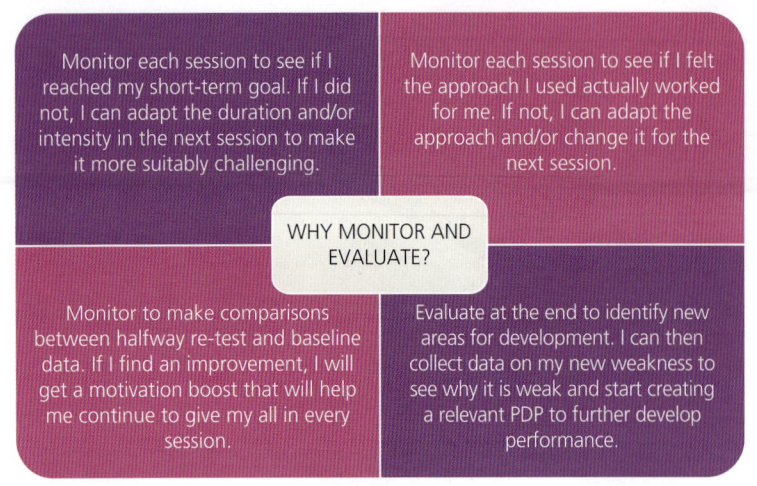

- Monitor each session to see if I reached my short-term goal. If I did not, I can adapt the duration and/or intensity in the next session to make it more suitably challenging.
- Monitor each session to see if I felt the approach I used actually worked for me. If not, I can adapt the approach and/or change it for the next session.
- Monitor to make comparisons between halfway re-test and baseline data. If I find an improvement, I will get a motivation boost that will help me continue to give my all in every session.
- Evaluate at the end to identify new areas for development. I can then collect data on my new weakness to see why it is weak and start creating a relevant PDP to further develop performance.

Figure 9.2

What is clear from monitoring is that it is all about assessing a session before, then planning what to do next. These changes are referred to as adaptations and they should only be made based on the thoughts and feelings the performer has from their last session.

> **TIP**
>
> For the Higher exam, you only need to know one monitoring method. By looking at the training diary, we are examining a method that can be used across all factors.

TASK 53 MATCH UP

Table 9.1 is a collection of thoughts and feelings and adaptations. Match them up to pick up 4 marks.

MONITORING REFLECTIONS	ADAPTATIONS
That interval training session was so boring.	In the next session, we will increase the number in our circle to create more problems.
The human knot was really easy.	In the next session, I will aim to achieve this in five reps as the last goal was too unrealistic.
I feel like I have mastered visualisation at home.	In the next session, I will add in a skill element to keep me motivated.
I failed to get calm inside three deep breaths today.	In the next session, I will try it at the training ground where there are more distractions.

Table 9.1

Monitoring method: training diary

Figure 9.3

It involves noting down a number of things in every session, including what you did and how you felt it went. Let's look at this monitoring method in relation to each command word.

BENEFITS   LIMITATIONS

- Easy to complete so you are unlikely to make mistakes.
- Allows you to write down your thoughts so you can see why something happened and make suitable adaptations.
- Is a permanent record so you can make comparisons between sessions.

- Validity can be questioned if not completed immediately

Figure 9.4

TASK 54 THE TRAINING DIARY AND COMMAND WORDS

1. Identify a method used to monitor your progress. (1)
2. Figure 9.5 outlines various aspects of a training diary. Identify those that relate to the description of the training diary. (3)

> I completed this method at the halfway point of my session and compared my scores to my baseline data.

> I chose this method because it was portable and I was able to take it to training with me.

> It is set out as a booklet with a page for every session of my PDP.

> I completed this method immediately after every session by stating what I did and how I felt it went.

> Based on my thoughts and feelings, I then wrote down my next steps and set a short-term goal for my next session.

> My coach told me my strengths before my weaknesses because they wanted to give me a confidence boost.

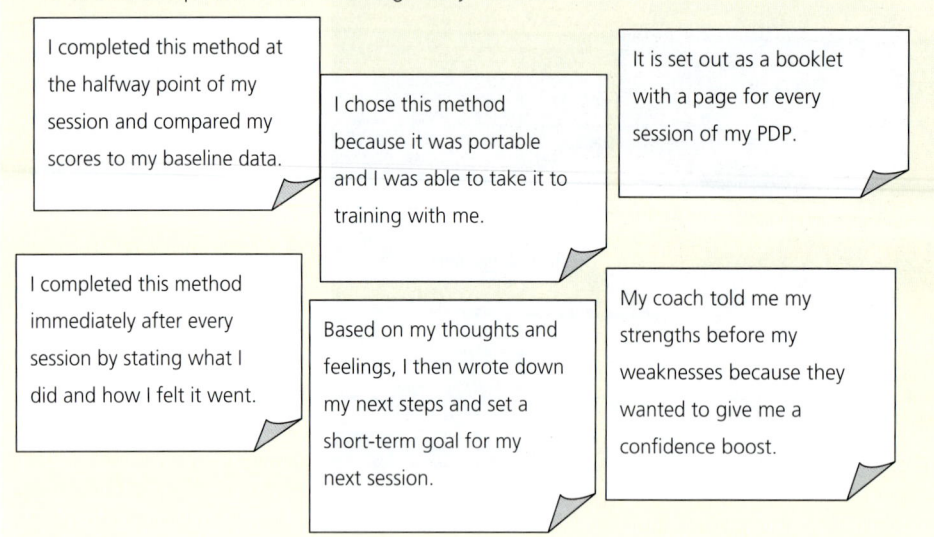

Figure 9.5

3. PEER HELPER: a Higher PE pupil often struggles with explanation questions because, although they are good at giving the cause, they cannot provide the effect to obtain a mark. Help them by finishing off their answers to pick up 2 marks. (2)

    I chose the training diary because it had a simple layout that was easy to complete. This meant…

    I also chose the training diary because I am able to write down how I felt a session went. This meant…

4. Upon evaluating the effectiveness of the training diary, a different Higher PE pupil has called it 'ineffective' *because my entries were not always accurate due to the memories of the session not being fresh in my head.* Why are the session details not always fresh in their head when completing the training diary? (1)

As discussed, one way to approach analysis answers is to provide a solution to a limitation of a method. Doing this will ensure that the process of completion will be more robust as you identify an important part of using this method. Consider this example analyse answer:

It is important that you complete the training diary immediately after each session. This is because you will actually be experiencing the thoughts of how the session went in your head at the time of writing. This means that your answer will be more accurate and can help you set the correct next steps.

So, why is this a good analyse answer?

a In sentence 1, there is clear evidence of the method being deconstructed: the important part of completing 'immediately after each session' is stated.

b In sentence 2, a valid reason is given for why this is important: 'actually be experiencing the thoughts of how the session went in your head.'
c In sentence 3, the impact this then has on the monitoring process is noted: 'answer will be more accurate and can help you set the correct next steps.'

Figure 9.6 offers a different point of analysis for you to consider.

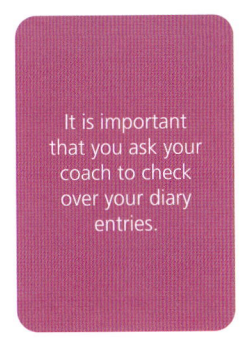

| It is important that you ask your coach to check over your diary entries. | This is because it can give you a different viewpoint as they can check it against how well they felt you did in the session. | This means your entries will be more reliable as you will be getting input from a more experienced person, who will discuss and confirm the accuracy of your notes. |

Figure 9.6

> 5 Using the analysis of the example answer above, now go through each of the three sentences in Figure 9.6 and give feedback on why each sentence is a good one. (3)

Evaluating method: re-test

At the end of your PDP, you will want to evaluate how effective it was in developing your identified weakness. To do this, it is worth doing a re-test. This is where you repeat the method you used to gather baseline data before your PDP. Once this is completed, a comparison can be made to evidence your progress.

Figure 9.7

> **TIP**
> Similarly to the monitoring method, you only need to know one method for evaluating the PDP. Be clever here and choose a re-test method such as the PPW because it covers all factors.

TASK 55 THE RE-TEST AND COMMAND WORDS

1. Identify a method used to evaluate the effectiveness of your personal development plan. (1)
2. When describing the re-test, you are essentially going through the same process of describing your data collection method BUT with an added feature: you must make reference to the timing of completion and the fact that you will compare it with your baseline scores. Focusing on the re-test of the PPW, delete the incorrect phrases in this paragraph. (4)

   I completed my PPW re-test before/after I completed my PDP. I did it in the exact same location/a different location as my baseline test by doing it at home on my own. I completed it by shading/placing tallies in a section with what I believed to be my score out of 10 in a 'sub-factor'. After completing the re-test, I handed it back to my teacher for them to assess/I compared my scores to my baseline data and measured if I had made any improvement.

> **TIP**
>
> Pupils sometimes get confused in these kinds of questions because they interpret evaluate as a command word. The command word is often at the start of the question. Evaluate is simply there because that is the name of the process in the cycle of analysis that we are investigating.

Providing it is done in the conditions described above, the re-test can be very beneficial for providing you with valid measurements of your progress.

TASK 53 MATCH UP

3. Match up the causes and effects below to build a 3-mark answer to the following question:

   Explain why you selected a certain method to evaluate your progress at the end of a personal development plan. (3)

CAUSE	EFFECT
Easy to complete having done it before.	Can measure progress in identified weakness and also identify new areas for development and start the cycle of analysis again to develop whole performance.
Using the PPW as a re-test allows you to measure progress in a range of 'sub-factors'.	Can easily measure the before and after figures to see if you have improved and reached your long-term goal.
Easy to interpret results.	Did not make any mistakes and therefore made more valid comparisons.

However, like all aspects of the course, there are some limitations to this method of evaluation. Figures 9.8 shows two of these limitations. Check them out before attempting the questions that follow.

LIMITATIONS OF THE RE-TEST

Using the PPW as a re-test method could be unreliable due to it using qualitative data.	If the performer is not in the same mood as they were on the baseline test it could lead to invalid comparisons being made.

Figure 9.8

4   a   A performer has evaluated that their re-test of the PPW was ineffective because they felt lower in confidence on the re-test than on the day of baseline data collection. Why would this be? (1)
    b   Why is collecting qualitative data as part of a re-test potentially problematic? (1)

Having considered the benefits and limitations of the re-test, let's analyse what makes the re-test work. Figures 9.9 and 9.10 outline two different important considerations a performer should bear in mind when using a re-test as a means of evaluating their progress.

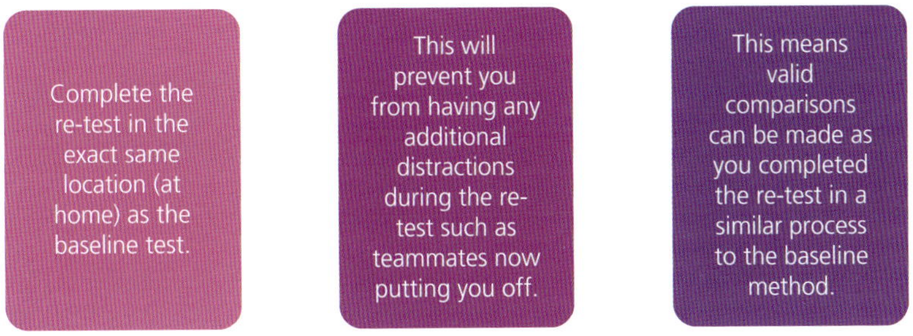

Complete the re-test in the exact same location (at home) as the baseline test. → This will prevent you from having any additional distractions during the re-test such as teammates now putting you off. → This means valid comparisons can be made as you completed the re-test in a similar process to the baseline method.

Figure 9.9

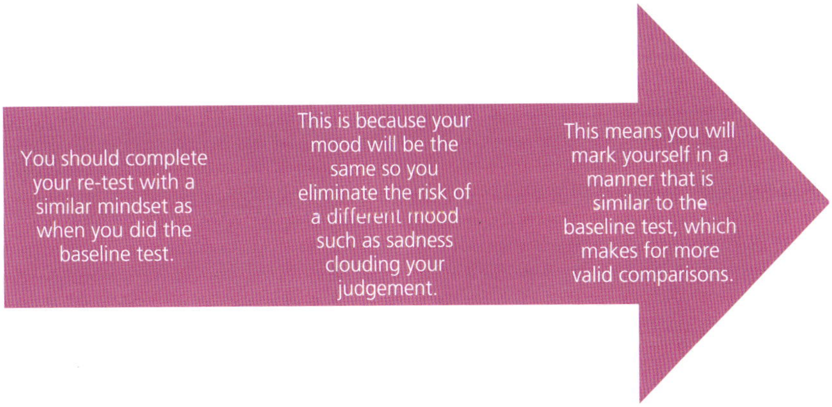

You should complete your re-test with a similar mindset as when you did the baseline test. → This is because your mood will be the same so you eliminate the risk of a different mood such as sadness clouding your judgement. → This means you will mark yourself in a manner that is similar to the baseline test, which makes for more valid comparisons.

Figure 9.10

5   Using these two analysis examples to guide you, analyse why it is important for a performer to ask their coach to check over their re-test results. In doing this, remember to provide a sentence that analyses:
    a   why this is important (1)
    b   the impact it then has on the evaluation process. (1)

Evaluating the effectiveness of a PDP

Having completed your PDP and evaluated how much you have improved personally, you may also wish to evaluate how effective the different parts of the PDP were. This is a question that pupils often struggle with in the National 5 portfolio and you may be asked something similar in the Higher exam.

When evaluating the effectiveness of your PDP, you can make reference to numerous different variables.

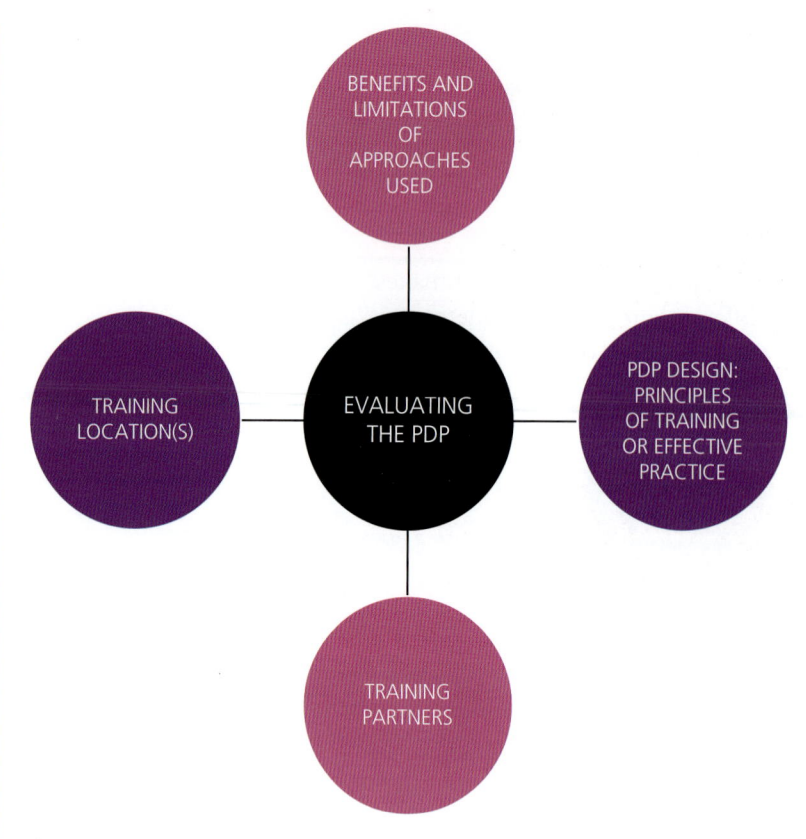

Figure 9.11

TASK 56 EVALUATING THE DIFFERENT PARTS OF THE PDP

1 Create a table with the following headings: PDP design, Approaches, Other.
2 Read the different answers in Figure 9.12 and place them in the correct column in the table. (4)
3 Pick one of these answers and finish off the evaluation. (1)

- Using the shadow practice in session 1 of my PDP was very effective because it suited me being at the cognitive stage of learning.

- Progressing the time of my interval training sessions from 20 minutes in session 4 to 23 minutes in session 5 was an effective part of my PDP.

- My PDP was effective due to it having a variety of approaches.

- Choosing to do visualisation at the training ground when doing it for the first time was an ineffective part of my PDP.

Figure 9.12

Identifying next steps

When evaluating progress at the end of a PDP, a performer can use the information they have obtained to help them identify their next steps. Some of the next steps open to performers can be seen in Figures 9.13 and 9.14.

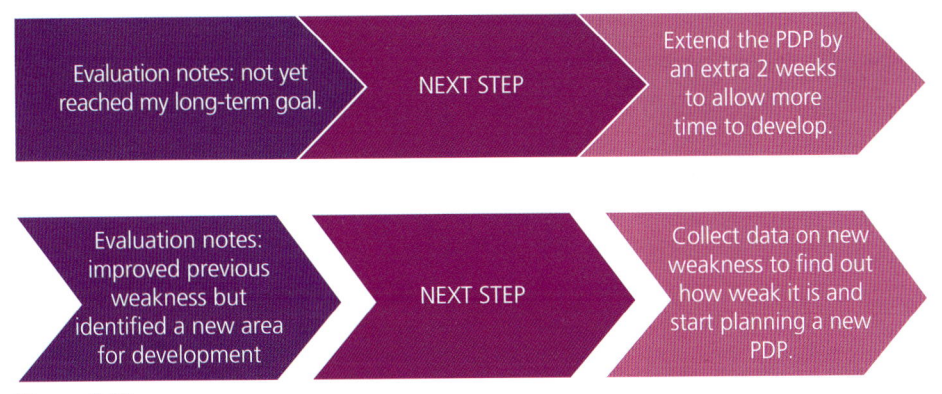

Evaluation notes: not yet reached my long-term goal. → NEXT STEP → Extend the PDP by an extra 2 weeks to allow more time to develop.

Evaluation notes: improved previous weakness but identified a new area for development → NEXT STEP → Collect data on new weakness to find out how weak it is and start planning a new PDP.

Figure 9.13

Evaluation notes: that approach was a very effective part of my PDP.

NEXT STEP

If the approach is suitable, include it as part of a new PDP that is developing a newly identified area of development.

Figure 9.14

TASK 57 NEXT STEPS

A Higher PE pupil has recently evaluated a mental PDP they did to control their anxieties. Below are their notes after completing an evaluation:

'I am much better at controlling my anxiety after scoring 7/10 in the re-test, whereas before it was 3/10.'

'In the PPW re-test, I only scored 2/10 for concentration.'

'I felt that deep breathing was a very effective approach for me.'

Q What are this pupil's next steps? (2)

CHAPTER SUMMARY

In summary, monitoring occurs throughout a PDP and helps a performer make suitable adaptations as they work their way through their programme. Evaluating occurs at the end of a PDP and involves making a judgement on your progress and supporting this with evidence.

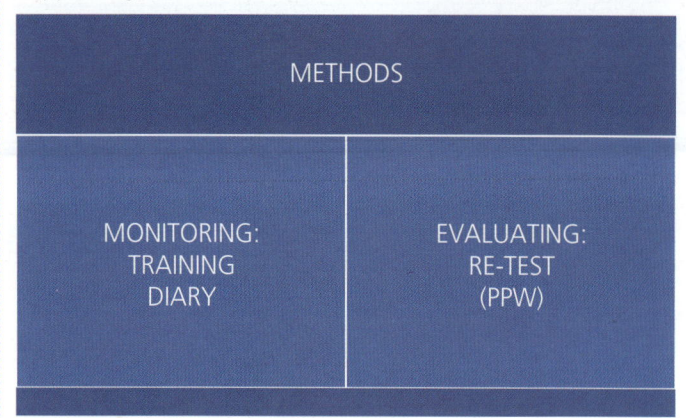

METHODS	
MONITORING: TRAINING DIARY	EVALUATING: RE-TEST (PPW)

Figure 9.15

EXAM-STYLE QUESTIONS

1. Explain why a performer should monitor their progress when completing a development plan for the physical factor. (3)
2. Describe a method used to monitor progress in the social factor. (4)
3. Analyse the method you referred to in Question 2. (2)
4. Evaluate how effective your personal development plan was for the emotional factor. (3)

TOTAL: ___/12

SCENARIO

10 Scenario

In section 3 of the exam, you will be presented with a scenario. A scenario takes any part of the Higher PE course content and frames it in a manner that requires you to use your problem-solving skills. The scenario will always relate to two factors and is scored out of 8–12 marks. Information will be given in different ways in a scenario, some of which can be seen in Figure 10.1.

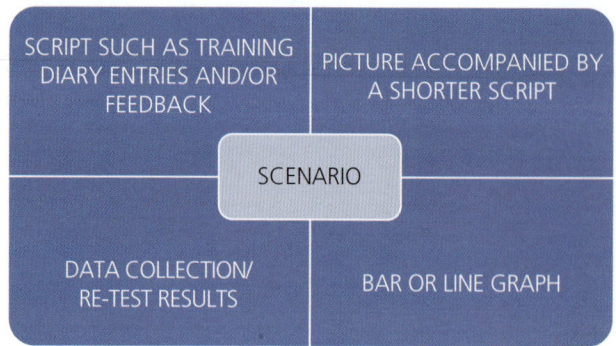

SCRIPT SUCH AS TRAINING DIARY ENTRIES AND/OR FEEDBACK	PICTURE ACCOMPANIED BY A SHORTER SCRIPT
DATA COLLECTION/ RE-TEST RESULTS	BAR OR LINE GRAPH

(centre: SCENARIO)

Figure 10.1

As stated previously, you must use your problem-solving skills when trying to interpret what a scenario is asking of you. One way to do this is to deconstruct the information provided into key terms and then annotate the scenario. Let's apply this technique to our mental scenario in Task 58.

TASK 58 MENTAL SCENARIO: SCRIPT*

Below is the diary entry of a Higher PE pupil after a performance.

Today's performance did not go to plan. I was extremely nervous throughout due to my friends watching me. At the start of my performance, I really struggled to focus. As I started to panic more, I then made a lot of poor decisions. Overall, a bad day at the office.

- activity
- anxiety
- concentration
- decision making
- negative

1 Analyse how mental factors brought about a reduction in this pupil's performance. (4)
2 Describe an approach this performer could use to develop their performance in the mental factor. (4)

*Note: our practice scenarios will relate to only one factor BUT the practice papers in the final chapter will provide you with scenarios containing two factors.

TASK 59 EMOTIONAL SCENARIO: BAR CHART

Figure 10.2 shows the results a Higher PE pupil obtained before and after completing a personal development plan for the emotional factor.

EMOTIONAL PDP: BEFORE AND AFTER

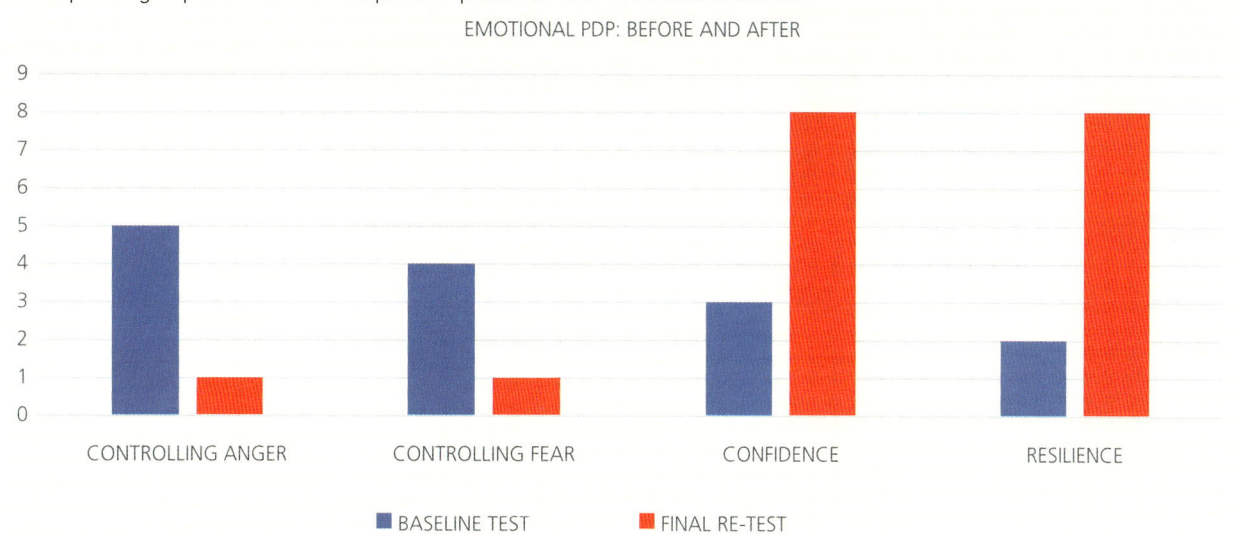

Sub-factor	Baseline Test	Final Re-test
Controlling Anger	5	1
Controlling Fear	4	1
Confidence	3	8
Resilience	2	8

Figure 10.2

> **TIP**
>
> Question 1 has more marks than the number of 'sub-factors' available in the scenario. In this case, you must show your breadth of knowledge by providing more than one example for some 'sub-factors'.

1 Evaluate how effective this pupil's performance is in the emotional factor having completed a personal development plan. (7)
2 Explain this pupil's next steps in the emotional factor. (1)

TASK 60 SOCIAL SCENARIO: DATA COLLECTION RESULTS

Below are a performer's results when collecting data on social factors.

STATEMENT	ANSWER
'I get on well with other members of my team.'	TRUE
'I can verbally express myself during a performance.'	FALSE
'I show respect towards opponents throughout a performance.'	TRUE

1 Explain reasons why a performer received these results when collecting data on the social factor. (5)
2 Explain what this performer may consider when creating a personal development plan to develop the social factor. (3)

TASK 61 PHYSICAL SCENARIO: PICTURE AND SHORT SCRIPT

Figure 10.3

'Performers who cannot maintain their energy levels towards the end of a performance are at a major disadvantage.'

1 Analyse how true this statement is in relation to the impact that physical factors can have on performance. (5)
2 A Higher PE pupil has discovered that the above statement is true of their physical capabilities and they are now considering collecting data on their performance levels. Explain reasons why they should collect data before starting a personal development plan. (3)

TEACHERS: PUTTING PEDAGOGICAL RESEARCH INTO PRACTICE

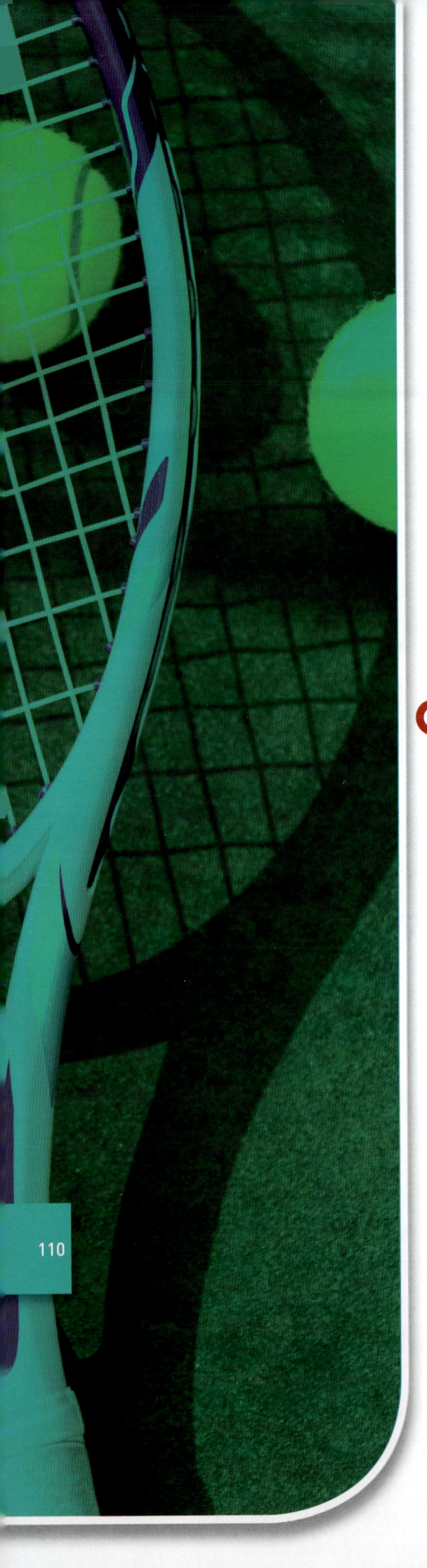

11 Teachers: putting pedagogical research into practice

This chapter is aimed solely at teachers. It gives you a range of fun and interactive exercises to use in the classroom environment. Each strategy stems from pedagogical research and will give you more ideas to use in theory lessons. Let's look at them in more detail.

Retrieval practice

When learning something new, we are taking in information and trying to store it in our memory. This will involve a variety of strategies such as reading, memorising, taking notes and much more. However, after we have covered content, we often forget it, or in time it does not feel as fluent as before. Retrieval practice combats this.

Retrieval practice refers to taking information from our long-term memory and bringing it to the forefront of our mind. In doing this, we are keeping information from previous lessons/terms fresh in our head, which consolidates knowledge and understanding.

> **TIP**
>
> Start your lessons with retrieval practice. Focus on content you have covered in the year so that pupils are having to retrieve and use it. Keep tasks small and specific; there is no need to ask pupils to answer an exam-style question here. For example: 'How many statements are in the SCAT questionnaire?' This could then lead to a greater discussion around this method of data collection.

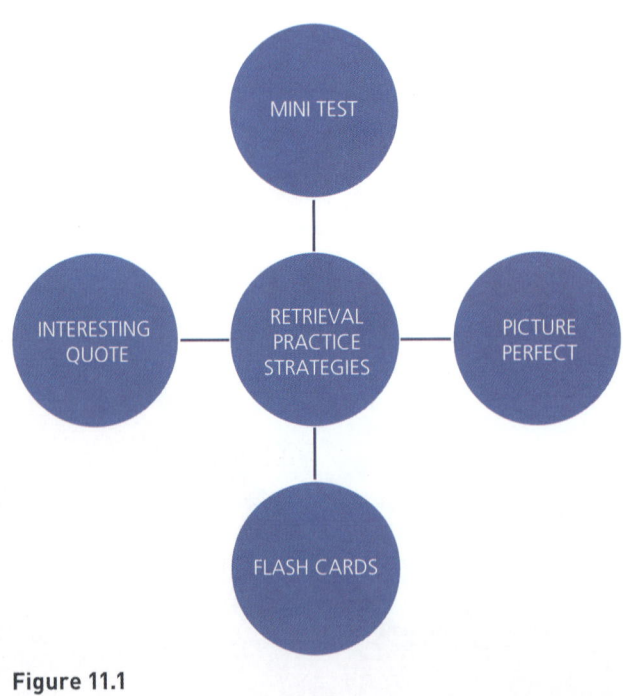

Figure 11.1

Examples

Let's pretend it is the first lesson in January and a class has covered the following content for all four factors:

- August–October: Data collection.
- October–December: Key planning information and Developing performance.

Mini test: five minutes to answer the questions

Figure 11.2

1. Describe how a method for the physical factor is set up. (2)
2. A pupil wishes to collect qualitative data for emotional factors because only they truly know how they feel. Explain the effect this could have. (1)
3. Evaluate one strength for the social factor against a model performer. (1)
4. Analyse one important part that makes a mental approach work. (1)

Picture perfect

Place a picture on the screen/board and ask pupils to note as much as they can about that topic inside a short amount of time. Allow pupils to be creative and take their notes in any format they wish. Once done, share it with someone in the class and compare and contrast notes.

Flash cards

Similar to 'Picture perfect': place a term on the screen and ask pupils to note down as much as they can about that topic. Leave the term on the screen for a short time before moving on to the next one. Try to stick to three per lesson, with each term representing a different course area.

Interesting quote

Put an intriguing quote on the board to cause some debate. Ask pupils to see to what extent they agree/disagree with the quote and to give reasons. This should be done on their own initially. Once done, place them into small groups to discuss opinions.

Continuous training is much better than interval training for developing CRE!

Co-operative learning

Co-operative learning involves pupils working with one another. The teacher places the class into small groups with a range of knowledge levels and abilities. The group members then work together and even split into pairs within the group to complete class tasks.

Some of the benefits of co-operative learning are:

- positive interdependence with the team working together to achieve a unified goal
- individual accountability which motivates pupils to 'do their bit' and put in the work as they are contributing towards the group effort
- holistically developing pupils as they learn how to respect people's opinions, listen when others are talking and provide feedback to one another
- developing critical thinking skills such as problem solving, decision making and creativity.

> **TIP**
>
> Before starting a co-operative learning model, go over non-negotiable social behaviours we expect to see in each team. Ask pupils to then make up their own three-point code of conduct and write it on the inside of their jotters.

Setting the scene

The homework approach

PUPILS	WEEK 1	WEEK 2	WEEK 3	WEEK 4	TOTAL
TEAM A					
A1					
A2					
A3					
A4					
TEAM B					
B1					
B2					
B3					
B4					
TEAM C					
C1					
C2					
C3					
C4					

When setting homework each week, give each pupil a personal score based upon effort. Maximum effort = 3 points; bare submission = 1 point; late/non-submission = −1 point. Each pupil's score then contributes to the team's weekly total. As the weeks go on, which team wins the homework competition at the end of term?

Scenario jigsaw puzzle

Figure 11.3

Give each team a scenario such as a set of data collection scores. Place enough scores in the scenario so that there is one score for each pupil to analyse.

Ask pupils to go over the scenario together as a group before each person takes a part of the jigsaw puzzle based upon their individual strengths. Once each pupil has written their answer, come together as a group and discuss the answers. Can pupils then feed back to one another to improve?

FACTOR	DATA COLLECTION SCORE 1 POOR TO 10 GOOD
Mental: concentration	8/10
Emotional: resilience	9/10
Social: communication	10/10
Physical: muscular endurance	2/10

An example question could be: Analyse why a pupil received these scores during their data collection block. (4)

One for me, one for you!

Place a question on the screen that has at least 4 marks. Split co-operative teams into partners within their group and ask them to work together to generate a full-mark response.

Then have the pairs play Rock–Paper–Scissors. The winner writes sentence 1 and sentence 3. The loser writes sentence 2 and sentence 4. Help is provided!

ADAPTATION: if describing a method of data collection, the winner writes how it looks/is set up and the loser writes how it is completed in chronological order.

Snowball fight

Organise teams into a competition format:

- Team A vs Team B
- Team C vs Team D

Using an A3 sheet of paper, ask each team to write down four questions. Each question must refer to either a different factor or a different part of the Cycle of Analysis. When they have finished, ask pupils to scrunch up their paper into a 'snowball' and wait for your command to throw it at the opposition team.

Figure 11.4

Once a snowball lands in a team's area, open it up and assign one question to each team member based on their strengths. The aim is to answer each question correctly before the other team then throws it back. Once back in the original area, they should mark the work in conjunction with you. Who gets the win? Change fixtures in a round robin format.

Google Maps

Figure 11.5

When learning how to describe, help pupils become familiar with making short, sharp statements without justification by using Google Maps.

Pupils work in pairs within their group and number themselves 1 and 2. Pupil 1 states a destination/room somewhere distant in the school. Pupil 2 must then list short, sharp directions for pupil 1 to get there in the most efficient manner.

Once they have finished, they should switch over.

*If comfortable with pupils doing so, let them walk it!

PE Pong

Figure 11.6

Each team has the following setup:

- Place four cups in a square on the table.
- In each cup there is a different question. These questions may range from easy to hard by following the command words or by looking at different course content.
- Give teams a hint about the question in each cup: 'Cup 1 has a question on monitoring and evaluating in it.'
- Pupils discuss, based on strengths, who will target which cup/question.
- Give each team a table tennis ball and ask them to try to throw the ball into their cup.
- Once the ball is in the cup, a designated pupil answers the question while others continue.
- There is a five-minute time limit: how many marks do they score?
- Move to the next table where a different set of questions awaits.
- At the end of the lesson, which team scores the most points?

Active learning

Active learning is not learning through practical performance; it can take place anywhere and does not necessarily involve movement. It places the pupil at the heart of the learning process and encourages them to do the following.

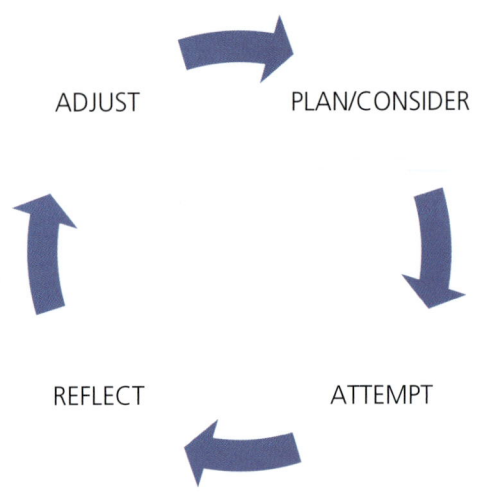

ADJUST → PLAN/CONSIDER → ATTEMPT → REFLECT → (cycle)

Figure 11.7

This ongoing cycle is best presented through open-ended tasks that involve pupils developing critical higher-order thinking skills such as analysing and problem solving. Having done this, pupils should be encouraged to collaborate and discuss their findings with others to help their reflections before attempting again (if required).

Let's look at some examples of active learning in action.

Think–Pair–Share

1. Pose a question or a statement to the class: 'Monitoring and evaluating are the same thing.'
2. Ask pupils to silently consider the extent to which they agree with this statement.
3. Before writing any answers, ask pupils to talk to the person next to them: Compare and contrast your thoughts.
4. Ask them to think more now about the discussion they have just had and share it with a different pair and/or the whole class.

Be the examiner

Figure 11.8

- Place an answer that ties in with the lesson content on the board. Deliberately ensure it is NOT full marks: if it is a 4-mark question, write a 2-mark response where there are two correct points and two incorrect points.
- If it is a describe question, throw in a 'why'/'justification' somewhere in the answer as opposed to a descriptive point OR make an incorrect statement.
- If it is an explain question, have a cause and effect that do not match OR place a cause without the effect.
- Get pupils to work individually: How many marks would you give this answer?
- Ask pupils to write down where they have awarded marks and give a reason why they awarded a mark.
- If a pupil has not awarded a mark, ask them to note down the reason and how the answer could be better to achieve a mark.
- Ask pupils to then pay attention to the board and compare/contrast with the teacher as part of a classroom discussion.

Peer marking

Figure 11.9

- Give pupils a question to attempt.
- Once they have finished, ask them to switch their answer with a partner and look up at the board where there is an evaluation sheet showing what should be in the answer OR create an evaluation sheet for pupils to work with and write on.
- Tell them to compare and contrast their partner's answer against the evaluation sheet.
- Where marks have been missed, ask pupils to consider how they could improve.
- Tell pupils to switch back and take turns to talk through each mark (not) awarded.
- Make changes if required.

*When you feel pupils are ready, get them to create their own 'mini test' and marking scheme that they can switch with another person in the class. This is a good way to differentiate for those needing an extra challenge.

REVISION PAPERS

Revision paper 1

> When attempting this paper as part of your revision, consider doing the following:
> - Annotate the paper: highlight key terms; re-word some confusing terms; note the marks.
> - Have a go at this paper without your notes initially.
> - Note down the questions you find tough, THEN revise them later.
> - Time yourself: you have 2 hours 30 minutes in the exam.

Section 1 (32)

1. a Describe a way you could receive feedback during a physical development plan. (5)
   b Analyse what should be considered when providing feedback on developing the physical factor in order for it to be considered useful. (3)
2. a Explain why a performer should collect data on their mental performance levels before creating a development plan. (4)
   b With reference to performance, evaluate the results a performer could receive when collecting data on mental factors. (4)
3. a Explain how social factors could impact performance development. (4)
   b i Describe the adaptations a performer could make while completing a social development plan. (2)
      ii Explain why they made these adaptations to their social training programme. (2)
4. a Explain why we should set goals during an emotional development plan. (3)
   b Describe what a performer may consider when setting goals for developing the emotional factor. (5)

Section 2 (8)

This part of the exam will look at personal development plans you completed in two factors.

Note down the two factors you developed at the top of your page for Section 2.

5 a Describe an approach you used to develop factor 1. (2)
   b Explain why you used this approach to develop factor 1. (2)
6 a Describe an approach you used to develop factor 2. (2)
   b Explain why you used this approach to develop factor 2. (2)

Section 3 (10)

Below is the feedback a performer received after completing both of their one-off performance activities.

Performance 1:

'It is clear that you are part of a very tight and supportive group. Throughout the performance, you worked well with others and showed respect to both your teammates and the opposition. Your teammates were always aware of where you were, based on your loud voice, and this contributed to a very successful performance. Well done.'

Performance 2:

'You appeared to be scared both at the start and throughout your performance. I thought you performed within yourself and did not maximise your potential. It was clear that you were not happy with this as you appeared to get frustrated when things were not going your way. Once this happened, there was no real evidence of you bouncing back and, unfortunately, it seemed to spiral out of control as the performance went on.'

7 a Evaluate this performer's performance levels in both assessments. Your answers must refer to emotional and social factors. (6)
   b In light of this feedback, explain what this performer's next steps might be in relation to emotional and social factors. (4)

Revision paper 2

> When attempting this paper as part of your revision, consider doing the following:
> - Annotate the paper: highlight key terms; re-word some confusing terms; note the marks.
> - Have a go at this paper without your notes initially.
> - Note down the questions you find tough, THEN revise them later.
> - Time yourself: you have 2 hours 30 minutes in the exam.

Section 1 (32)

1. a Describe an analytical tool used to obtain information on physical factors. (6)
   b Explain why a performer may use quantitative data to collect methods on physical factors. (2)
2. a Explain why it is important to monitor and evaluate progress in social factors. (3)
   b Describe a method used to record information on your progress in social factors. (5)
3. a Evaluate how effective your performance was in emotional factors. (5)
   b Analyse how emotional factors can link to any other factor during performance. (3)
4. a Explain how mental factors could impact performance development. (2)
   b Describe an approach used to develop performance in the mental factor. (6)

Section 2 (10)

This part of the exam will look at personal development plans you completed in two factors.

Note down the two factors you developed at the top of your page for Section 2.

5
- a Explain what you considered when creating a development plan for factor 1. (2)
- b Describe any adaptations you made to your development plan for factor 1. (2)
- c Explain why you made one of these changes to your development plan for factor 1. (1)

6 a Explain what you considered when creating a development plan for factor 2. (2)
- b Describe any adaptations you made to your development plan for factor 2. (2)
- c Explain why you made one of these changes to your development plan for factor 2. (1)

Section 3 (8)

Below is a comparison of the results a performer obtained before, during and after two different development plans.

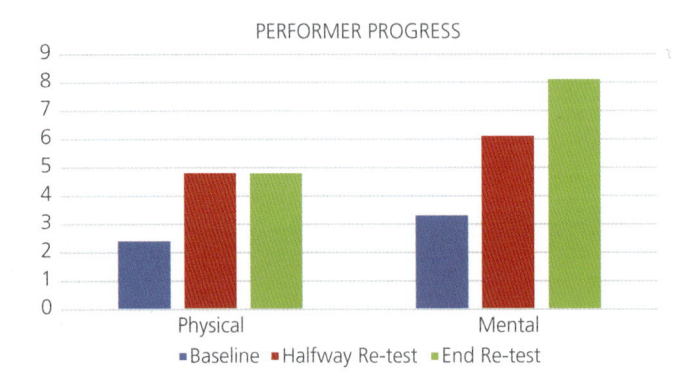

PERFORMER PROGRESS

7 a With reference to the development plans, analyse possible reasons why a performer saw this progress in the physical and mental factors. (4)
- b With reference to performance, evaluate how effective this performer was when performing in both the physical and mental factors after completing their development plans. (4)

ANSWERS

Chapter 3 Answers: Factors impacting performance

TASK 1 Sub-factors buzz words

'SUB-FACTOR'	BUZZ WORD(S)
Anger	Frustrated
Communication	Called loudly
Decision making	Chose
Width	Wings
CRE	Tired
Resilience	Bounced back
Etiquette	Sportsmanship
Anxiety	Nervous

OPTIONAL TASK Sub-factors buzz words

'SUB-FACTOR'	BUZZ WORD(S)
Confidence	Self-belief; believed in myself
Team dynamics	Chemistry; support; encouraged
Concentration	Focus; blocked out
Accuracy	Precise; on target

TASK 2 Build the answer: anxiety

SPECIFIC SITUATION	IMPACT ON PERFORMER	IMPACT ON PERFORMANCE
I was anxious when serving against a break point in tennis.	This meant my palms started to sweat and my grip on the racquet was weak.	This resulted in me making a poor connection with the serve, which lacked power and hit the net.
I was anxious when taking a penalty kick in rugby.	This meant the muscles in my legs started to tense up and my movements became rigid.	As a result, my kick lacked power and missed as it fell short of the posts.
I was anxious when putting to win a matchplay tie in golf.	This meant my body started to shake as I gripped the putter.	This led to me hitting the ball with the wrong part of the putter and my putt missed as it lacked accuracy.

TASK 3 Guided discovery task: concentration

1 When you are in the games hall playing badminton, there is a high chance that there are other matches taking place on courts around you. You need to focus on the flight of the shuttle on your court and block out the noise from other courts. This will allow you to track the shuttle's flight through the air effectively and get into position to make the return.

2 When you are man-marking in basketball, there will be other players moving around you on court. You must focus on the person you are marking and not become distracted by the movements of others. This will allow you to stay close to your opponent and intercept passes made to them.

TASK 4 Shot placement: decision making

a I used my decision making during a tennis rally when my opponent was at the back of the court.
b This meant I decided to play a drop shot to the space at the front of the court.
c This resulted in me winning the point as my opponent could not reach the ball before it bounced twice.

Task 5 Read the green

1 I would strike the ball firmly and aim it slightly to the right.
2 This means it would have enough power to get up the hill and by going slightly to the right it can come back round towards the hole as it hill slants to the left.

This results in the ball following a logical path to the hole and going in.

TASK 6 Fill in the blanks: anger

I got angry in basketball after the referee made a call I disagreed with. This meant that I got so frustrated that I started to **shout and swear** at them. This resulted in me being **ejected from the game** and my team playing with one player less.

I also got angry in golf after I missed an easy putt to make par. This meant that I was so angry that I tried to hit my next drive with **far too much force**. This resulted in me **losing control of my shot** and it going out of bounds.

TASK 7 Be the examiner: confidence

Sentence 1 is very good because it paints a clear picture of the situation: *it tells us when in volleyball the performer lacked confidence.*

Sentence 2 is not so good because it is **not specific** in telling us exactly what a lack of 'self-belief' did to the performer: **did they doubt themselves and not fully commit to the serve, for example?**

Sentence 3 is good because it provides a *specific and logical* impact on performance. *It does not go off on tangents.*

TASK 8 Personalised resilience answer

a I showed my resilience after I missed an easy smash at the net in badminton.
b This meant that I managed to forget about the error and focus my attention on the next point.
c This resulted in me being aggressive in the next point and not being scared to take on the smash when the opportunity arose to win the rally.

Task 9 Trusting my teammates

The performer's lack of trust in their teammate's abilities could have a negative impact on performance during a dance routine. This means that the performer will not believe in their teammates abilities to stay in time and will lose focus as they keep their eye on them. This could result in the performer getting their own footwork wrong as they are so concerned about their teammate that they do not fulfil their own responsibilities.

TASK 10 Colour code: communication

Communicated when setting the ball up to teammate in volleyball.	Shouted the direction for the team to move in as the opponents passed the ball.	My teammate was ready and set to perform an accurate spike.
Communicated when organising our zonal defence in handball.	Shouting my teammate's name to alert them to the incoming pass.	Stayed unified and moved as a unit to minimise gaps for opponents to shoot.

TASK 11 Etiquette examples

a Examples of etiquette occurring in different activities are:
- shaking hands with opponents at the end of a basketball match
- applauding a good shot from an opponent in badminton.

b I demonstrated high levels of etiquette when my opponent performed an excellent drop shot against me in badminton. This meant that I applauded their effort and complemented their drop shot. As a result, the respect between us grew and the match was played in a fair and sporting manner.

TASK 12 'Sub-factor' pinball: team dynamics

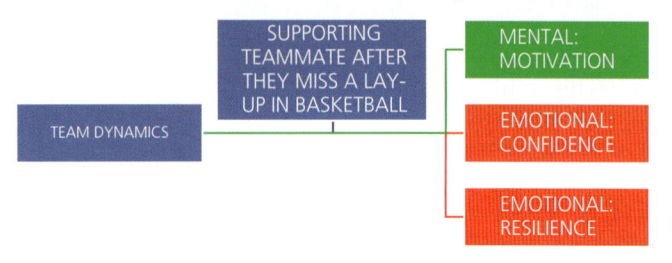

```
TEAM DYNAMICS ─── SUPPORTING TEAMMATE AFTER THEY MISS A LAY-UP IN BASKETBALL ─┬─ MENTAL: MOTIVATION
                                                                               ├─ EMOTIONAL: CONFIDENCE
                                                                               └─ EMOTIONAL: RESILIENCE
```

a Motivation, confidence and resilience

b High levels of team dynamics helped my teammate after they missed an open lay-up in basketball. This meant that we supported and encouraged them to forget about the miss and move on. This resulted in their motivation levels increasing as they did not want to let us down and they gave 100% to fulfil their role and responsibilities.

Task 13 Feeling excluded: inclusion

This resulted in the opposition easily anticipating where the ball was always going and made interceptions to stop our attack before performing a fast break against us.

TASK 14 Match-up: accuracy

Inaccurate dig in volleyball.	Ball goes behind teammate and out of play for a point to the opposition.
Inaccurate shot in hockey.	Ball does not go far enough into the corner and is close to the goalkeeper who saves it.
Inaccurate lob in tennis.	Ball is hit with too much power and lands out at the back of the court.
Inaccurate drive in golf.	Ball does not follow a straight line and goes off to the side and lands out of bounds.

a High levels of accuracy helped me when making a through pass in football. This meant that I played a precise pass between the opposition's two centre backs. This resulted in my teammate reaching the through ball behind the centre backs and into a one vs one situation with the goalkeeper.

TASK 15 Past paper question: CRE

More errors could have been observed in the final five minutes of a handball match because the performer had low CRE levels. This meant that they were very tired and their skill level started to drop. As a result, they started to make inaccurate passes that were easily intercepted by the opposition, who went on to punish them by scoring.

TASK 16 Spot the difference: width

a   Answer B.
    Answer B is better because:
    - Sentence 1 in Answer B is more specific in stating how width was achieved: 'wingers stay wide to the touchline'. Answer A, however, just says that 'width was really helpful'.
    - Sentence 2 in Answer B is more specific and detailed in saying where space was created: 'spaces to open up in the centre of the court.' Answer A simply says 'space was created for others'.
    - Answer B contains a logical impact on performance with the 'pivot getting into spaces and shooting'. Answer A does not provide any impact on performance to finish off the answer.

Task 17 Picture perfect

Power helped me when performing in the high jump at my school sports day. This meant that in my approach I was able to run as fast as I could and then take off explosively from my right foot. This resulted in me generating a lot of height and cleanly going over the bar to move to the next height.

EXAM-STYLE QUESTIONS

1   Being unable to control my anxiety hindered my performance when taking a penalty kick in football. This meant that my leg muscles started to tense up and my movements became rigid. This resulted in my strike lacking power or accuracy and the goalkeeper making an easy save.
    High levels of concentration helped my performance when man-marking in basketball. This meant I focused on the player I was marking and blocked out the movements of others around me. This resulted in me staying tight to my opponent and intercepting passes towards them.
2   Being able to communicate was helpful when the ball landed between my partner and me in doubles tennis. This meant that I shouted my name loudly to inform them that I would play the shot. This alleviated any potential confusion and resulted in them moving out of the way to give me time and space to execute an accurate return.
    Poor team dynamics hindered our performance when in an attacking two vs one in handball. This meant that rather than pass the ball to my teammate who was in a better position than me, I decided to go alone because I did not like them and did not want them getting credit from our coach. This resulted in me being tackled by the opponent and the chance to score was lost, with arguments then breaking out between us.
3   I failed to control my anger when my team were losing an important match in rugby. This meant that I got frustrated and committed a dangerously high tackle on an opponent. This led to me being red-carded and leaving my team a player down on the pitch. As a result, they had to cover more ground and their CRE levels deteriorated, causing them to concede a match-winning try in the final five minutes of play.

Chapter 4 Answers: Data collection

TASK 18 Closed reading: data types

1. Questionnaire.
2. A performer may wish to collect qualitative data on emotional factors because only the performer themselves truly knows how they feel in relation to 'sub-factors' such as confidence and sadness. This means that they can accurately identify their own emotional strengths and weaknesses and create a PDP specific to their areas of development.
3. Standardised fitness test.
4. A performer may wish to collect quantitative data on physical factors because it provides them with a numerical score in the bleep test. This means they can use this score to set a realistic target for their PDP to develop their CRE levels.

TASK 19 Sticky notes: PARV(M)

PRACTICAL	APPROPRIATE	RELIABLE	VALID	MEASURABLE
I chose the PPW because it was easy to interpret my results. This meant I was able to identify my weaknesses and create a relevant PDP.	I chose the bleep test because it has been proven to collect data on CRE levels. This meant I trusted the protocols and carried it out properly to obtain a result I could compare to research-informed NORMS to help me set realistic targets.	I chose the general observation schedule because I was able to collect data across three matches. This meant I got a realistic overview of my abilities and was able to trust the data to identify my skill level and pick an appropriate approach for my first session.	I chose the questionnaire because the questions were easy to understand. This meant I knew exactly what the questions were asking of me and I answered them correctly.	I chose the communication observation schedule because I was able to store the results. This meant I could compare them to my re-test results to measure my progress.

TASK 20 The PPW and command words

1. PPW.
2. Inside each of the 8 sections are 10 segments that range from 1 (weak) to 10 (strong).
3. Descriptive bullet points:
   - I completed the PPW at home on my own with all electronic devices turned off.
   - I considered my score out of 10 in a mental 'sub-factor' and shaded in the appropriate number of segments.
   - I then repeated this for each of the other 7 mental 'sub-factors' and identified my highest and lowest scores.

4   I chose the PPW because it was practical as it was easy to interpret my strengths and weaknesses. This meant I was able to select appropriate mental approaches to include in my PDP for my identified weakness. For example: visualisation to aid my concentration.

5   The PPW could be ineffective because it requires the performer's opinion when scoring themselves. This would be ineffective if the performer lied about their performance levels to impress their coach so they did not get dropped for an upcoming match. As a result, their score would be inaccurate and unreliable.

6

DECONSTRUCT: Complete the PPW the same day of a performance.

WHY?: Memories of the performance fresh in head.

IMPACT: Easily recall information and accurately score yourself in each section.

TASK 21 The questionnaire and command words

1   Sport emotion questionnaire.
2   a False: it has 22 emotive terms.
    b True.
    c False: circle a number between 0 and 4.
    d False: complete it on the same day as a performance.
3

CAUSE	EFFECT
I chose the sport emotion questionnaire because it was practical as it was easy to complete.	This meant the memories of my performance were fresh in my head and I was able to accurately complete the questionnaire.
I chose the sport emotion questionnaire because it was valid as I was able to complete it on the same day of my performance.	This meant I was able to compare my baseline results to my re-test results to see if I was improving during my PDP.
I chose the sport emotion questionnaire because it was measurable as it was a permanent record.	This meant I made no mistakes in an easy process and my answers were correct.

4   The limitation in this question should not be matched up with the green answer in the answer table above because it contradicts itself with accurate data vs inaccurate data. It could therefore be matched up with either the yellow answer (practical – easy to complete) or the blue answer (measurable – permanent record).

5

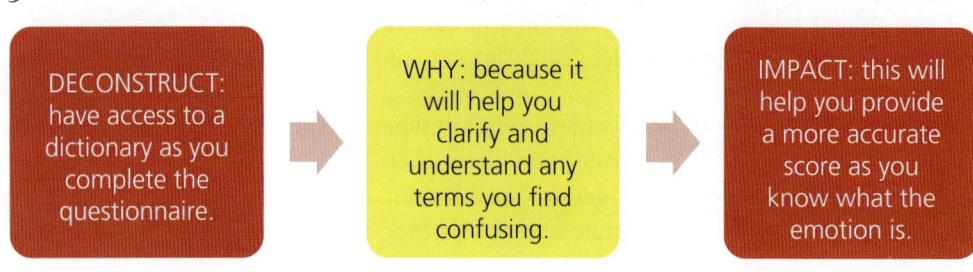

| DECONSTRUCT: have access to a dictionary as you complete the questionnaire. | → | WHY: because it will help you clarify and understand any terms you find confusing. | → | IMPACT: this will help you provide a more accurate score as you know what the emotion is. |

TASK 22 The communication observation schedule and command words

1. Communication observation schedule.
2. - *I would pick* any classmate available *to watch my performance and tally whether I did or did not perform each form of communication.* The performer should pick a knowledgeable classmate to observe them and complete the observation schedule.
   - *I would have them do this across three games* because it makes my data reliable *as it rules out a 'fluke' performance.* With describe answers, do not justify anything. Simply get to the point and move on to the next point. The examiner does not need to know the 'why'.
3. A) This means my partner is unlikely to make any mistakes and the data will be filled out correctly.
   B) This means I can get a true picture of my performance as it minimises the risk of a fluke performance in one game.
   C) This means I can compare my re-test results to my baseline results to see if I have improved.
4. a The communication observation schedule was ineffective when I was observed playing against a team that was much better than ours. This was ineffective because our team had much less possession of the ball and I could not use a variety of the communication skills I normally would. As a result, I did not get a true overview of my communication skills.
   b The communication observation schedule was ineffective because it was time-consuming being marked across three games. This was ineffective because my partner who was marking me started to get bored and lost concentration. As a result, they missed some aspects of my performance and my data was not completely accurate.
5.

DECONSTRUCT	WHY	IMPACT ON DATA
Combine the observation schedule with digital analysis.	Understand what each form of communication looks/sounds like in the context of the activity.	Fill out the table correctly to provide a more accurate overview of your strengths and weaknesses.
Have a knowledgeable partner observe your performance.	Overcome the fast-paced nature of the game to ensure nothing is missed.	Get the full picture of performance, which increases the reliability of results.

TASK 23 The standardised fitness test and command words

1 Standardised fitness test (bleep test).
2 The bleep test has two cones set up 20 metres apart in the games hall.
3 The pupil's statement is incorrect as it is not any two bleeps. It should read that a performer is out when they miss two consecutive bleeps.
4 A. This means I can use the score I achieve to help set my initial training sessions at the correct intensity and/or duration.
   B. This means I can use the score to help me set a realistic long-term target for my physical PDP.
   C. Measurable: my bleep test score can be noted down and stored as a permanent record.
5 Although the bleep test provides you with a numerical score, it could be ineffective because a performer may be influenced by their peers when completing the test. This could be ineffective because they may simply drop out when their friends drop out as they are embarrassed to be running in front of them. As a result, their score would be inaccurate and unreliable.
6

Have two people measure out the 20m for the bleep test.	This is because you can double-check that the distance has been measured correctly.	This means you will be following the protocols correctly and can obtain a valid result.
Have a partner tally your score as you complete the bleep test.	This is because you may lose count of your score during the test.	This means your partner will ensure you get the accurate point at which you drop out of the test and you will get a reliable result.

TASK 24 The GOS and command words

1 General observation schedule (GOS).
2

DESCRIBING THE GOS

WHAT DOES THE METHOD LOOK LIKE? (1)
The GOS is a table with six badminton skills along the top and two rows for effective and ineffective down the left-hand side.

WHO IS INVOLVED IN THE PROCESS? (2)
A knowledgeable partner is asked to observe your performance and mark the GOS.

I was observed playing against badminton opponents who were of a similar ability to me.

WHEN: IS THIS JUST A ONE-OFF OR COLLECTED OVER A CERTAIN TIME PERIOD? (1)
My partner observed me play three badminton matches.

HOW IS THIS METHOD FILLED IN? (1)
My partner watched me play and placed a tally mark in the appropriate box.
For example, if I won a point with a smash, a tally was placed in the 'effective smash' box.

3 I chose the GOS because it was practical as it was easy to interpret my results. This meant I was able to identify my strongest and weakest skills, then create an appropriate PDP to improve my weakness.

I also chose the GOS because it was practical as it was easy for my partner to complete. This meant they made no mistakes in an easy process and the data I received was accurate and correct.

Finally, I chose the GOS because it was valid as I played against an opponent who had similar levels of ability to mine. This meant that I was able to show my 'normal' performance levels as I took on a challenge I would normally face and this gave a realistic overview of my skill levels in badminton.

4

BENEFITS	LIMITATIONS
Practical: easy to complete – no mistakes – correct data.	Time-consuming gathering data across three matches – switch off and miss data.
Measurable: permanent record – compare to re-test results – measure progress.	Fast-paced nature of the game – miss shots – do not get the full picture.

5 WHY: This is because if you only collected data in one game, you may have an 'off' performance and not play to your usual standards.
IMPACT: This means that you wouldn't get an accurate overview of your performance levels in badminton and your results would be unreliable.

TASK 25 Digital analysis and command words

1 Digital analysis.
2 Answers that are weaker and should be deleted are highlighted.

- The iPad was placed at the side of the games hall at ground level on the centre line. VERSUS The iPad was placed high up on a stand at one end of the games hall.
- A match against a team of similar ability level was recorded on the iPad. VERSUS A match against a team of lesser ability was recorded on the iPad.
- After the match, the coach watched the video alone and provided the team with verbal feedback on their strengths and weaknesses. VERSUS After the match, the coach watched the video and provided the team with verbal feedback on their performance as they showed them when the strengths and weaknesses occurred.

3 Our team used digital analysis to collect data on our tactical performance because it captured the whole performance. This meant that despite the fast-paced nature of the game, everything was captured and we could reliably identify all the strengths and weaknesses in our performance.

Our team used digital analysis to collect data on our tactical performance because we were able to use functions like slow motion and pause. This meant our coach was able to look in depth at each strength and weakness to see why they occurred before giving more accurate feedback.

4 Digital analysis was slightly effective in gathering data on our tactical performance. It was effective because we were able to use functions like slow motion and pause. This was effective because our coach was able to look in depth at our strengths and weaknesses to see why they occurred before giving more accurate feedback. This then allowed us to focus specifically on our weaknesses by picking relevant approaches in our first training session.

However, it was ineffective because it can be time-consuming watching a full performance back. This was ineffective because when we were receiving our feedback, there was such a high volume that we switched off and stopped paying attention. This then resulted in us not picking up on all of our weaknesses that needed correcting and we only partially improved our performance.

5

DECONSTRUCT
- You need to ensure that the iPad is positioned high up when recording the game.
- The footage in the digital analysis should be analysed by a knowledgeable other such as the coach.

WHY?
- This is because they will truly understand what a strength or weakness looks like.
- This is because the camera is positioned in a manner that it provides a clear overview of the full court, meaning nothing is missed.

IMPACT
- This means that the data analysed will be reliable as you get the full picture.
- This means they can then complete the analysis correctly and give you accurate feedback.

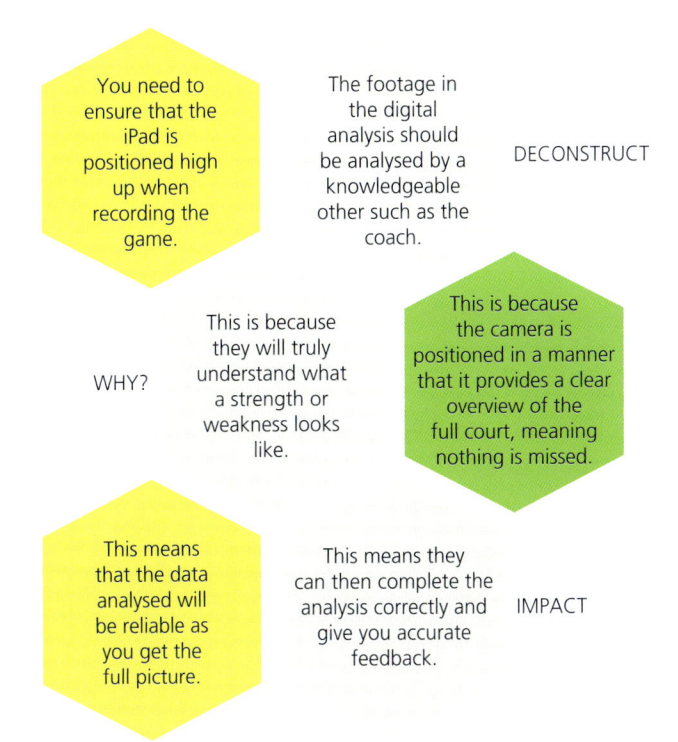

TASK 26

Mental factors

Like a model performer, I am good at controlling my anxiety levels when taking a penalty kick in football. This means that similarly to my model performer, I am capable of staying calm and keeping my leg muscles relaxed rather than tensing up. As a result, we are both capable of hitting our penalties with power and scoring.

However, unlike a model performer, I have poor concentration levels when marking at corners in football. This means that while a model performer maintains their focus, I often get distracted and start ball-watching rather than concentrating on the opponent I am marking. This results in my opponent getting away from me and having a free header at goal.

Emotional factors

Like a model performer, I have very high resilience levels and can bounce back after I make a double fault in tennis. This means that like my model performer, I can forget about the error and regain my composure before the next serve. As a result, I am then able to switch my focus to the sub-routines of my upcoming serve and perform it accurately.

However, unlike a model performer, I sometimes have very low levels of confidence when I am losing in tennis. This means that unlike my model performer, I lack belief in my abilities and play safe with every shot because I am scared of making unforced errors. As a result, I simply hit shots down the middle and allow my opponent to take the initiative and move me around the court.

Social factors

Like a model performer, I demonstrated good sportsmanship and etiquette when my opponent hit a good shot in badminton. This means that like my model performer, I applauded my opponent when they hit an excellent drop shot during a rally in our match. This resulted in respect growing between us and the match being played in a respectful manner.

However, unlike a model performer, I had poor communication skills when a shuttle was about to land between my partner and me in doubles badminton. This meant that unlike my model performer, I failed to call my name to alert my partner that I would play the shot. As a result, both of us went to play the shot and we collided with one another, failing to return the shuttle over the net.

Physical factors

Like a model performer, I have very good CRE levels in the final quarter of basketball matches. This meant that like my model performer, I had enough energy to keep up with the opponent I was marking when they tried to get away from me. As a result, this saw me deny them space and mark them out of the game so they could not receive a pass.

However, unlike a model performer, my passing in basketball is poor and lacks accuracy. This means that unlike my model performer, I often play passes behind my teammates and they cannot receive the ball. As a result, this leads to my stray passes going to the opposition, who can break on us.

TASK 27 Recap

1. False.
2. You would not use the same model performer for every factor because there are very few athletes who excel in each of the four factors. For example, Serena Williams is excellent in the physical factor, but she has weaknesses within the emotional factor. As a result, we should try to pick certain athletes who excel specifically in one factor as our model performers.
3. Focused observation schedule.
4. A pupil should make continuous reference to their chosen model performer. This can be as simple as saying 'like my model performer' or 'unlike my model performer'. They should also start by giving a judgement on their selected 'sub-factor' before providing the evidence to support this.
5. A pupil may not want to pick an elite athlete as their model performer because they are unlikely to reach their standards. This means that they could lose confidence and motivation and give up when they see that they are never reaching their model performer's levels.
6. A pupil may use a classmate as a model performer because it will give them a visual of what high performance of a skill or technique actually looks like. This means they can easily identify how a sub-routine is a strength and then make more valid comparisons to their own performance while using it to improve performance.
   A pupil may also use a classmate as a model performer because it can give them a motivation boost seeing someone in their class performing to a high standard. This means they will feel 'if they can do it, then so can I', which will give them the desire to start training and improve.

EXAM-STYLE QUESTIONS

1. A performer should collect data before beginning a social PDP because it will allow them to identify their social strengths and weaknesses. This means that the performer can then create a relevant PDP for their social weaknesses and include appropriate approaches to develop them.
   A performer should also collect data before starting a social PDP because it provides them with a baseline measurement of their starting abilities. This means that the performer can compare this result to their re-test scores to measure their progress and improvement.
2. A performer may wish to collect quantitative data on their performance in the physical factor because it will give them a statistical and numerical score like in the bleep test. This means they can then use this score to set realistic long-term goals for their CRE PDP, which can give them a boost in motivation to start their PDP.
3. A qualitative method used to collect data on mental factors is the performance profiling wheel (PPW). The PPW is a circle that is divided into 8 sections with 10 segments inside each section. On the outside of each section is a mental 'sub-factor' chosen by the performer. They rate themselves out of 10 in each section. With 1 being weak and 10 being strong, the performer would shade in the number of segments that indicate their score in each section. The performer would complete this method at home on their own with all electronic devices turned off.
4. Sport emotion questionnaire.
5. The sport emotion questionnaire should be completed by a performer at home on their own. This is because they will have no teammates watching them who may judge them when rating themselves. As a result, the performer is likely to be more honest, which will lead to them obtaining accurate results.

The sport emotion questionnaire should also be completed on the same day of a performance. This is because the memories of the performance will be fresh in the performer's head, meaning they can clearly relate the emotive terms to elements of their performance. As a result, the performer can be more accurate in completing the questionnaire, which will provide them with reliable results.

6 Like a model performer, I perform a broad range of skills and techniques in badminton with a high degree of accuracy. This means that like a model performer, I can perform skills like a drop shot with precision and land it just over the net. This results in me winning a number of rallies when my opponent is at the back of the court as my opponent cannot reach the shuttle in time.
However, unlike a model performer, I have poor CRE levels and I start to tire in the final set of badminton matches. This means that unlike a model performer, I am unable to keep up with the pace of play and struggle to return shots that are placed into spaces away from me. This results in my opponent exploiting my fatigue and moving me around the court to win more points.

Chapter 5 Answers: Feedback

TASK 28 Intrinsic or extrinsic

1 C
2 A
3 E
4 D
5 B

TASK 29 Usefulness of feedback

SOURCE: Feedback on performance in the physical factor can be considered useful when it is delivered by a coach as opposed to a classmate. This means that the feedback is likely to be accurate due to the high knowledge and experience levels a coach has, which will make it more trustworthy.

TIMING: Feedback on performance in the physical factor can be considered useful when it is delivered immediately after a performance. This means that the performance will be fresh in a performer's head, which will help them make sense of the incoming feedback.

ORDER: Feedback on performance in the physical factor can be considered useful when the coach outlines the positives before the negatives. This means the performer will likely feel a confidence and motivation boost, which will make them more inclined to listen to the negatives and strategies to improve them.

VOLUME: Feedback on performance in the physical factor can be considered useful when it is delivered in short and sharp bursts. This means the performer will not be overloaded with information and will be able to fully take on board the points given to them to develop their performance.

Chapter 6 Answers: Key planning information

TASK 30 Data analysis

Anxiety.

TASK 31 Process of elimination

1 Having identified that I cannot control my anxiety levels, I have decided to create a PDP on improving this 'sub-factor'. In this PDP, I am going to include approaches such as positive self-talk/deep breathing to improve this weakness. Having scored 1 out of 10 in my baseline measurement, I am going to set a goal of 5 out of 10 by the end of my 3-week PDP.
2 9/10 is far too high a goal and is not realistic for this pupil. Could result in a loss of motivation when they realise it is not attainable.

TASK 32 Goal setting

CAUSE	EFFECT
Set goals to give us a motivation boost.	By checking if we are achieving each short-term goal, it lets us know if and/or how we can adapt the next session to ensure we are suitably challenged.
Set goals to give each session a specific focus.	Give 100% in every session to ensure that we reach our goals and improve.
Set goals to aid monitoring and tracking processes.	Helps our partner, who is watching our session, by giving them a specific area to feed back on to let us know if we are on track to meet our short-term goal.

TASK 33 Deconstruction

By the end of today's session, I want to control any anger I may feel inside 8 deep breaths.

1 SPECIFIC: sub-factor ('anger') and reference to approach ('deep breaths') both stated.
2 MEASURABLE: a clear figure ('8') is provided.
3 REALISTIC: a realistic figure ('8') is provided after the previous achievement of 10 was achieved. Note: we want to control anger quicker so the progression goes down.
4 TIME: a clear deadline ('end of today's session') is established. This is also correct as end of the session suits a short-term deadline.

TASK 34 Incorporating the principles of training

PRINCIPLE OF TRAINING	EXAMPLE IN A PDP
SPECIFICITY	A tennis player prefers to include interval training in their PDP as opposed to continuous training because it contains different paces, like in a match.
PROGRESSION	A football player felt that their last two sessions were not challenging enough. As a result, they have asked their coach to make the duration of their next approach longer.*
OVERLOAD	A badminton player has decided to push themselves and will increase how often they train in a week from twice a week to three times a week.*
REVERSIBILITY	In week 3 of their PDP, a dancer trained four days in a row and now feels exhausted. In week 4, they plan to train Monday, Wednesday, Friday and Sunday so they have a rest in between each day to minimise the risk of injury.
TEDIUM	A gymnast decides to use a variety of CRE approaches rather than doing the same one over and over again.

*The progression and overload answers could be switched.

TASK 35 Stages of learning

1. Relying fully on kinaesthetic feedback at the cognitive stage could be problematic because the performer does not have a full understanding of how the skill should feel or look at this point. This means they will not have the experience or knowledge like a coach to know whether the skill is being performed correctly and therefore they will not give themselves the correct feedback to help progress their performance.
2. Errors will occur using the combination drill because they have yet to master the sub-routines of the overhead clear at the cognitive stage. This means that their performance of this skill will include numerous mistakes and will not flow correctly, which will mean that they cannot perform combinations with different skills.

TASK 36 Principles of effective practice

PRINCIPLE OF EFFECTIVE PRACTICE	EXAMPLE
Variety	I made session 4 tougher than session 3 by adding in a hoop to the back of the court where I wanted the shuttle to land during my repetition drills.
Progression	After completing session 3, I discovered that my goal was far too easy, so I decided to make it harder and more realistic to my ability levels in session 4.
Specificity	I always finished each session with some sort of fun game to give me something to look forward to at the end.
Measurable	When learning the overhead clear, I decided to use a range of approaches like shadow practices, repetition drills and pressure drills to keep things interesting.
Achievable	I decided to make my repetition drill more game-like by instructing my partner to feed the shuttle to the back of the court while I was standing at the front when learning the overhead clear.
Realistic	I noted my thoughts and feelings of each session in my training diary and then used this to help me set the correct next steps.

PRINCIPLE OF EFFECTIVE PRACTICE	EXAMPLE
Time	When I reached the autonomous stage, I decided to move to conditioned games so that I can learn how to make decisions about when and where to use the overhead clear in matches.
Exciting	I decided to make session 1 just 15 minutes long when doing the shadow practice because I was aware that it could get boring performing without the use of a shuttle.
Recorded	In session 4, I wanted at least eight of my overhead clears to land in the targeted area.

EXAM-STYLE QUESTIONS

1. A performer should set goals before their social PDP because it will give them a motivation boost so long as they are realistic. This means they will give 100% in every session in order to achieve their goals and improve their communication skills.

   A performer should also set goals during a social PDP because it will aid their monitoring and tracking processes. This means that by checking if they reached each session's short-term goal, they can then increase or decrease the demands in their next social session in order to ensure this session is at a challenging level for them.

2. By the end of my six-week mental PDP, I would like to achieve a score of 7/10 for controlling my anxieties in my PPW re-test. OR (if relating to activity) By the end of my six-week mental PDP, I would like to control my anxieties and remain calm when taking a free throw in basketball.

3. By the end of today's session, I want to be more resilient and forget about any mistake I make
   in the conditioned game after two phrases of positive self-talk.

4. PRINCIPLES OF TRAINING: a performer should consider making their CRE PDP specific to their activity of netball. This is because by selecting approaches such as interval training, they can develop their CRE levels while mirroring the stop-start nature of a netball match. This can result in them not only lasting a full match but also being able to move at different paces to fulfil their role and responsibilities while playing as a centre.

   A performer should also consider progressing their CRE PDP as they move through their plan. This is because it will ensure that they continue to challenge and push their CRE levels. This can result in them avoiding hitting a plateau and continuing to improve towards the achievement of their long-term goal.

   A performer should consider adding in rest days to their session to avoid reversibility. This is because if they train every day without rest, they run the risk of picking up an injury. By adding in a rest day to overcome this, the performer could then attend sessions in a good physical condition and perform at a higher standard to reach each session's short-term goal.

   PRINCIPLES OF EFFECTIVE PRACTICE: a performer should consider using a variety of approaches in their lay-up PDP. This is because it will ensure each training session is different, which could make it more enjoyable. This can result in the performer feeling more motivated to attend training and to then give their all to ensure they improve their lay-up.

   A performer should also consider making their lay-up PDP specific to their cognitive stage of learning. This is because they can then select approaches such as

the shadow practice and access external feedback from a knowledgeable other like their coach to ensure they build good movement habits. This can result in them building their confidence when initially learning the
lay-up and suitably prepare them for more demanding tasks as they move into the associative stage of learning.

Finally, a performer should make their lay-up PDP exciting by adding in a game at the end of each session. This is because it will give them something to look forward to as they work their way through a monotonous approach such as a repetition drill. This can result in them staying focused and mentally tough during these difficult moments in order to achieve their session goal before taking part in the game at the end.

Chapter 7 Answers: Developing performance

TASK 37 Fill in the blanks: approaches

An **approach** is the name given to a drill we use to develop our performance. To develop my ability in the mental factor, I will use **deep breathing**. This will help me **control my anxieties** and improve my **focus**. For the **social** factor, I will use team-building games to help develop my **communication** skills and our **team's dynamics**. In the emotional factor, I can develop my confidence levels by **visualising** myself performing successfully. In the physical factor, the three different elements can be developed with specific factors; for my CRE, I will use **interval training**; accuracy will be developed with **repetition drills** and our team's **width** in attack can be developed with **unopposed practices**.

TASK 38 Deep breathing and command words

1. Deep breathing.
2. I initially used deep breathing at home on my own. I did this because I did not want to have teammates watching me and potentially embarrassing me for using such an approach. I also did it initially with all electronic devices turned off just to help ensure I remained fully concentrated when doing it. I breathed in through my nose for 4 seconds, then held it for 2 seconds before breathing out through my mouth for 4 seconds. This counted as 1 deep breath and I repeated this another 4 times. In my next session, I progressed the approach by reducing the number of deep breaths from 5 to 3 because I would not have long to regain my focus during a game due to its fast-paced nature.
3. I used deep breathing because I have watched a number of elite athletes using it during high-pressure situations. This meant that I trusted this approach and took it seriously by fully concentrating on mastering it and doing it correctly to help me control my anxieties.
4. Deep breathing was very effective in helping me control my anxieties when taking a penalty pass in netball. This was effective because taking a few deep breaths helped calm me down and relax both my mind and body before executing the shot. As a result, I scored as my muscles felt relaxed so my movements were fluid and the shot had the power and accuracy to go into the goal, whereas the muscular tension has caused my shot to miss in the past.
5. a A performer should decrease their repetitions as they master deep breathing because their ultimate aim is to use it in game situations, where time is often limited.
   b As a result, a performer will work on reducing their anxieties quickly, so they no longer impact their performance in a negative manner.

TASK 39 Visualisation and command words

1. Visualisation.
2. Marks would be awarded for:
   - I initially completed this approach at home on my own with all electronic devices turned off.
   - I visualised myself scoring a variety of different goals whilst including the sounds of the crowd and the sight of the opponents trying to put me off.
   - I repeated these images 5 times each and reduced the number of reps to 4 in my next session.
3. In sentence 1, the pupil is simply introducing the approach without describing any aspect of it. In sentences 3 and 5, the pupil is justifying why they used the approach as opposed to describing it, and would therefore not be awarded marks.
4.
   - Used by elite athletes: This meant that I fully trusted the usefulness of the approach and gave it my all in order to master it and use it effectively.
   - Requires no equipment: This meant that I wasted no time setting things up and I was able to maximise time spent on the approach and mastering it.
5. Visualisation was slightly effective in boosting my confidence in the emotional factor. It was beneficial because I was able to complete it anywhere. This was good because when I first started using it, I was able to do it at home, which enabled me to take my time and use it correctly without anyone judging me. This resulted in me mastering the approach over time before I was then able to take it into a live performance.
   However, the time taken to master it was a limitation because I was not able to use it in a fast-paced situation immediately. This was limited because it did not give me an immediate confidence boost when using it in performance because I was too slow in visualising myself being successful. This resulted in me initially performing without confidence as I could not use it efficiently due to the time taken to visualise myself being successful.
6.

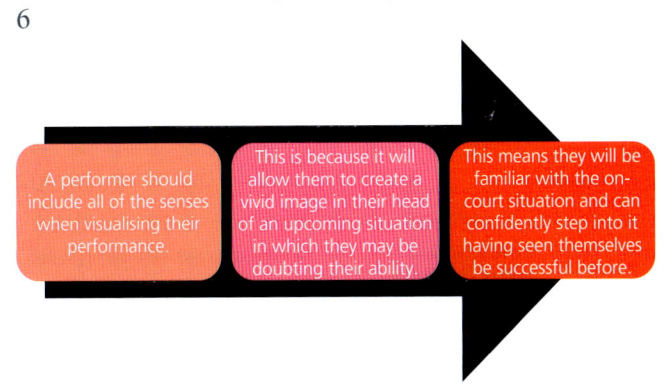

   [Arrow diagram with three boxes:]
   - A performer should include all of the senses when visualising their performance.
   - This is because it will allow them to create a vivid image in their head of an upcoming situation in which they may be doubting their ability.
   - This means they will be familiar with the on-court situation and can confidently step into it having seen themselves be successful before.

TASK 40 Team-building games and command words

1. Team-building games (human knot).
2.
   a. 8.
   b. False: they grab the hand of somebody who is not standing next to them.
   c. The group must break up and start the whole process again.
   d. When the whole group has untangled the knots and are standing in a clear circle.
   e. It can be progressed by increasing the number of participants from 8 to 10.

3

Cause	Effect
I chose the human knot because it required no equipment.	This meant we were able to get into the approach quickly and work on developing our team dynamics rather than wasting time setting things up.
I chose the human knot because it forced us to communicate to solve the problem of untangling the knot.	This meant we became familiar with voicing our opinions and issuing instructions which we were then able to take on to the pitch.
I chose the human knot because it was fun.	This meant we enjoyed working together and our team dynamics grew as we looked forward to taking part in these sessions.

4 Possible answers include:

Team-building games really improved my communication skills when my team had possession in football. This was because I have now started asking for the ball more loudly and often when I am in space and my teammate has the ball. This has resulted in me receiving the ball more often in the final third and creating more chances, as opposed to before, when I stayed quiet and did not receive the ball as much.

Team-building games really improved my communication skills when my teammate had possession of the ball in handball. This was because I am now much better at alerting them to an opponent chasing them by shouting 'man on' more often. This has resulted in our team being slightly better at maintaining possession as they release the ball before they are dispossessed, whereas before, I would have stayed quiet even though I saw them being closed down.

Team-building games really improved my communication skills when we were using zonal defence in basketball. This was because I am now shouting the direction we should move in in relation to the opposition's use of the ball more often. This has resulted in our team staying more unified and closer together when using zonal defence, whereas before we were too open due to a lack of communication and cohesion.

5

It is important that you complete team building games with a variety of different teammates.

This is because it will allow you to communicate and build relationships with everyone in your team.

This means that you will be able to work with, and support, all of your teammates on court, regardless of your position or whether subs have been made.

It is important that any team building game contains a problem that needs to be solved.

This is because it will force your team to communicate and work together in order to achieve the task.

This means you will be able to collaborate together on court to overcome any problems that arise during a performance.

TASK 41 Interval training and command words

1. Interval training.
2.

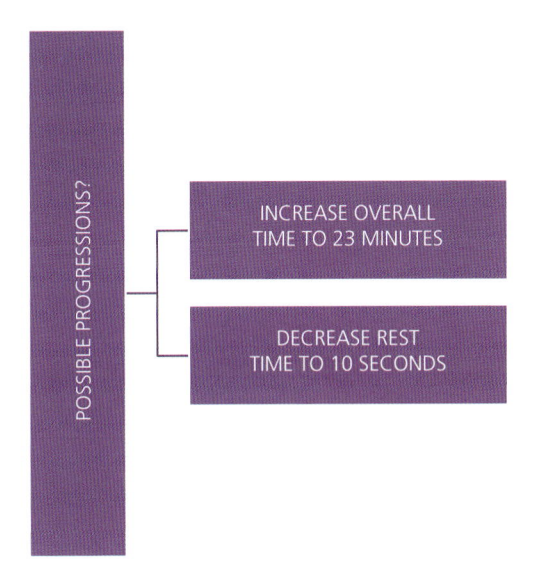

POSSIBLE PROGRESSIONS?
- INCREASE OVERALL TIME TO 23 MINUTES
- DECREASE REST TIME TO 10 SECONDS

3. a Paragraph 2 picks up a mark because the cause and effect fit together:
I also chose interval training to develop my CRE levels because it was specific to my activity, netball. This meant that the constant changing of pace mirrored what happens in a netball match and I developed my CRE in a way that it helped me fulfil my specific role and responsibilities.

   b Paragraphs 1 and 3 do not have matching causes and effects. The effects in each of these paragraphs should be switched in order to access 3/3.

4. Interval training could be limited because it can get boring working between two paces for a prolonged period of time. This means I could lose motivation and stop working hard during my session, which results in no improvement or attainment of my short-term goal.

5. a Evaluate the effectiveness of an approach used to develop physical factors.
   b Evaluate how effective an approach was in developing your physical performance.

6. The key difference in these questions is that one is looking at the benefits and limitations of an approach while the other is concerned with the changes it brought about in performance.
   a Evaluate the effectiveness of an approach you used to develop the physical factor.
   b Evaluate how effective an approach was in developing your performance in the physical factor.

7. It is important that you select a training partner with similar CRE levels to yours when completing interval training. This is because it can add in a realistic level of competition to your session as you go at approximately the same pace. This means it will motivate both of you to work hard to keep up with one another and therefore develop your CRE levels.

TASK 42 Shadow practice and command words

1 Shadow practice.
2 The descriptive points relevant to the shadow practice are:

I pretended to perform a smash over and over again while using no equipment. After each attempt, I received feedback from my coach on the way I performed different sub-routines. I completed this approach for 3 sets of 10 repetitions during my session. This approach was progressed by increasing the number of repetitions to 12 in each of the 3 sets.

3 Matching causes and effects:

- Does not require any equipment — Maximise training time working on developing skilled movement rather than setting things up.
- Can obtain feedback after each attempt — Immediately understand if on the right lines or not and make corrections straight away if necessary to develop good habits.
- Easy to progress

4 a 'ineffective due to how tedious it was.'
   b 'as the session went on … start to get bored at not being able to hit the shuttle.'
   c 'losing motivation in the final set.'

5

- You should add in game-related movements prior to the shadowed skill movements in each rep.
- This is because it will overcome the tedious nature of simply shadowing a skill as it makes it more game-related.
- This means you can remain motivated as you learn more about where and when the skill can be used in a game, which will boost your efforts in training.

TASK 43 unopposed practice and command words

1 Unopposed practice.
2 a Pupil A: 2 marks. Pupil B: 1 mark.
   b Pupil A: *In this, we got into our positions on the pitch and walked through how we wanted to move the ball from the goalkeeper to the striker.* Pupil B: *Throughout the approach, our coach gave us a combination of video and verbal feedback by showing us what we did well and how we needed to improve.*

c Pupil A did not get a mark for the following sentence because they are justifying why something happened in the unopposed practice as opposed to describing a part of it: *We did this without any pressure because we wanted to master our movements before trying it out in a game.* Pupil. B did not get a mark for the following sentence because they have started to evaluate an effective part of the approach rather than describing how it was completed: *This was effective because it allowed us to learn our movements and the options open to us when we were in these situations in games.*

3 EFFECT 1: This means performers can learn about the strategy without any pressure, which can help them focus fully on learning their roles and responsibilities within the strategy.
EFFECT 2: This means the coach can correct errors as soon as they occur, which prevents any bad habits from developing.

4 CAUSE and EFFECT 1 can be matched with LIMITATION 2: Unopposed practices were effective because we were able to learn a new strategy without the presence of any opposition. This was effective because we were able to focus fully on our role and responsibilities within the strategy without fear of making mistakes. This resulted in us fully understanding what was expected of us and we were able to implement the strategy successfully.

However, unopposed practices were limited because the coach kept stepping in to provide feedback. This was ineffective because our session never truly flowed and we started to get slightly frustrated at the constant interruptions. This resulted in us taking longer to learn the strategy and it was not as enjoyable as it could have been.

CAUSE and EFFECT 2 can be matched with LIMITATION 1: Unopposed practices were effective because our coach was able to give us regular feedback during the session. This was effective because we were quickly made aware of any mistakes we made during the practice. As a result, these mistakes were eradicated, and we built up good habits.

However, unopposed practices were limited because the lack of opposition made it quite boring. This meant some of us started to lose motivation and did not focus as well as we could have done. This resulted in our effort levels being lower and we did not implement the strategy as well as we could have done.

5 a

DECONSTRUCT	WHY	IMPACT
The coach should provide ongoing feedback throughout the unopposed practice.	This is because it will make the practice more exciting and make the performers more motivated when completing the approach.	This means good habits can be formed as mistakes are eradicated and the players will be suitably prepared to try this strategy with some opposition.
The coach could add in a points system upon completing each repetition of the unopposed practice.	This is because your players are still learning how to implement the strategy and will ultimately make mistakes.	This means they will be more focused during the session and try harder in order to achieve more points, which ultimately sees them train better.

b Adding in the points system during the practice can help overcome the tedious nature of the unopposed practice.

EXAM-STYLE QUESTIONS

1. An approach I used to develop my communication skills for the social factor was team-building games (human knot). In this approach, I got into a group of six people and we formed a circle in the games hall. We all then placed our right hand in and grabbed the hand of somebody who was not standing next to us. We then repeated this process with our left hand but also grabbed somebody different from the first time and again, someone who was not standing next to us. On the teacher's whistle, we attempted to untangle the knot without breaking links until we formed a clear circle. (Marks could also be awarded for describing what happens if links are broken and/or how the approach was progressed.)

2. I used visualisation to help boost my confidence in the emotional factor because it required no equipment to complete. This meant that I wasted no time setting things up and maximised my training time visualising seeing myself being successful over and over again.

    I also used visualisation because it could be completed anywhere. This meant that I was able to complete it at home initially when I was still inexperienced and master it without distractions before trying it in game situations.

3. When using deep breathing to help me control my anxieties for the mental factor, it was important that I gradually decreased the number of repetitions as I started to get better at it. This was because I ultimately wanted to use it in game situations where time is in short supply. This meant that I learnt how to control my anxieties quickly and use it in high-pressure situations as they occurred.

    It was also important during that deep breathing that I tensed my muscles when breathing in and relaxed them when breathing out. This meant that as well as controlling my cognitive anxieties, I was able to flush out any somatic anxieties I was starting to experience. This meant that my breathing pattern helped keep my muscles relaxed, which helped maintain my power and accuracy in skills I was executing.

4. a Interval training was slightly effective as an approach in developing my CRE.

    It was effective because it was easy to progress the intensity of my sessions. This was effective because I was able to reduce the rest periods in my next session, which enabled me to work harder. This resulted in me continuing to improve my CRE levels while avoiding hitting any plateau in my development.

    It was ineffective because it did start to become a bit tedious. After a while, I started to lose motivation without having any sort of skill involvement within the session. As a result, my effort levels weren't as high as they could have been and although I did improve my CRE, it was not to the standard I could have reached.

    b Interval training was very effective in helping develop my performance in basketball.

    It was effective because it saw my CRE levels improve in the final quarter of my match when we were on the fast break. This was effective because I still had the energy to change pace and accelerate forward to support my teammates. As a result, we managed to create an overload and used the extra player to score a basket, whereas before, I would have been far too tired to make this run.

    It was also effective because it helped my CRE levels improve in the final quarter when I was man-marking my opponent. This was effective because when they tried to accelerate away from me, I was also able to accelerate and stay close to them. This resulted in them being marked out of the game and our team eventually regained possession, whereas before, that opponent would have got away from me and scored, with me being too tired to keep up.

Chapter 8 Answers: Factors impacting performance development

TASK 44 Concentration

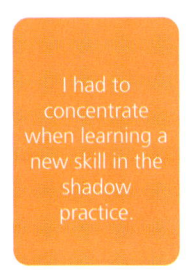

I had to concentrate when learning a new skill in the shadow practice. ➡ This meant that I was able to focus on one sub-routine at a time while blocking out the noise from other people practising around me. ➡ This resulted in me building up the appropriate muscle memory and reaching my short-term goal.

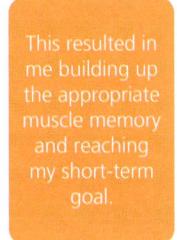

TASK 45 Be the examiner: motivation

a The pupil gives a specific situation when they were lacking motivation in interval training: 'halfway through'.
b 'Started to get bored'; 'no longer wanted to continue'.
c The pupil's answer is better because they said exactly what happened during the session to cause their CRE to not improve as desired: 'not working as hard as I could'.

TASK 46 Anger

I struggled to control my anger when I made several mistakes when practising a spike during repetition drills. This meant that I got so frustrated that I lost my focus and composure. As a result, I stopped focusing on my sub-routines and continued to hit poor spikes without improving.

TASK 47 Resilience

SPECIFIC SITUATION	IMPACT ON PERFORMER	IMPACT ON TRAINING
Being resilient helped my team after we made the wrong move in the human knot.	As a result, we stuck together and made the correct next move, which helped us move forward in fully untangling ourselves.	This meant that we bounced back from the error by reflecting on why it went wrong and explored different moves.
Having high levels of resilience helped me after I missed a lay-up in a repetition drill.	This meant that I bounced back by seeking feedback from my coach on why I missed rather than dwelling on it.	This resulted in me really focusing on my footwork on the approach to the basket and being more accurate in my next attempt.

TASK 48 Communication

I used my communication skills to offer my opinions when solving the problem of untangling the human knot. This meant that I clearly said what to do and provided my reasons on why it would be the correct next move. This resulted in us then discussing it as a group and following my advice to move closer to untangling the knot.

TASK 49 Fill in the blanks: co-operation

My co-operation skills enabled me to *support* my partner when they were doing extra practice on their drop shot in badminton. This meant I *gave up my time* to stay behind with them and *provide them with feeds* to the back of the court. This resulted in their extra practice *being more game-like* due to my feeds and they developed their drop shot.

My partner showed excellent co-operation skills when I was struggling to bench press in a weights training session. This meant that they *assisted* me by spotting my reps and *giving me encouragement* when I was tiring to push the bar up. This resulted in me feeling more *motivated* to push through the pain and less *fearful* of hurting myself as I knew they were there to help me improve my strength.

TASK 50 Accuracy

My lack of accuracy hindered my partner's development when they were trying to improve their smash in a repetition drill.

This meant that my feeds were never set up well for my partner as they were not left hanging high at the net for them to smash.

This resulted in my partner not having as many opportunities to develop their smash and the muscle memory that goes with it.

TASK 51 Muscular endurance

a Answer A: arms and shoulders helped me in the final set.
   Answer B: my legs did not help my teammates' performance in goals
b Answer A: arms and shoulders remained fresh.
   Answer B: my legs were too tired.
c In Answer A, the pupil was able to continue practising their sub-routines in each rep to improve, while in Answer B, the goalkeeper in the pupil's team did not get tested as much and did not improve their reflexes.

EXAM-STYLE QUESTIONS

1 Being able to concentrate helped me when attempting deep breathing during a high-pressure moment in a conditioned game. This meant that I was able to focus on counting my breaths in and out while blocking out those talking around me. This resulted in me staying calm and focusing on my sub-routine to get double points.
2 I failed to control my anger when my teammates were messing around during team-building games. This meant I got so frustrated that I started shouting and criticising them. This resulted in arguments breaking out and we fell out rather than forming closer relationships.

3. My teammate demonstrated their co-operation skills by helping me learn their position during an unopposed practice while they were out injured. This meant that they gave me advice and instructions on when and where to move to as the strategy progressed. This resulted in me improving my knowledge and helping my team learn the new strategy quickly.
4. High levels of accuracy helped me be an effective feeder for my partner during a repetition drill. This meant that my feeds went high to the back of the court when they were learning how to perform the overhead clear. This resulted in them being able to execute a higher number of repetitions under game-like pressure and improving their overhead clear.

Chapter 9 Answers: Monitoring and evaluating

TASK 52 Fill in the blanks

Monitoring occurs **during** a PDP, whereas evaluating occurs at the **end** of the PDP.

Monitoring involves you looking back after **each session** to see how it went: what were the **positives and negatives** of the session? From here, **adaptations** can be made to ensure the PDP continues to provide you with an appropriate challenge.

Evaluating involves **judging** how effective the PDP was in developing your performance. It helps you answer questions such as: Did I reach my **long-term goal**? Do I have any new **development areas** that I can take back through the Cycle of Analysis? Doing all of this will help you make a suitable judgement on the effectiveness of your PDP.

TASK 53 Match up

MONITORING REFLECTIONS	ADAPTATIONS
That interval training session was so boring.	In the next session, I will add in a skill element to keep me interested.
The human knot was really easy.	In the next session, we will increase the number in our circle to create more problems.
I feel like I have mastered visualisation in the house.	In the next session, I will try it at the training ground where there are more distractions.
I failed to get calm inside three deep breaths today.	In the next session, I will aim to achieve this is five reps as the last goal was too unrealistic.

TASK 54 The training diary and command words

1 Training diary.
2 It is set out as a booklet with a page for every session of my PDP. I completed this method immediately after every session by stating what I did and how I felt it went. Based on my thoughts and feelings, I then wrote down my next steps and set a short-term goal for my next session.
3 I chose the training diary because it had a simple layout that was easy to complete. This meant that I made no mistakes filling it out so each of my entries was correct. I also chose the training diary because I am able to write down how I felt a session went. This meants that I can then use these thoughts and feelings to plan my appropriate next steps for the following session.
4 Their entries are unlikely to be accurate because it sounds as though they are completing the training diary some time after their training session as opposed to immediately afterwards. Therefore, the memories of the session will not be fresh in their head.

5 In sentence 1, the method has been clearly deconstructed with an important part identified: 'ask your coach to check over your diary entries.'
   In sentence 2, there is a valid reason given as to why this is important: receive a 'different viewpoint as they can check it against how well they felt you did in the session'.
   In sentence 3, there is a clear impact on the monitoring process with 'entries will be more reliable as you will be getting input from a more experienced person who will discuss and confirm the accuracy of your notes'.

TASK 55 The re-test and command words

1 Re-test (PPW).
2 I completed my PPW re-test after I completed my PDP. I did it in the exact same location as my baseline test by doing it at home on my own. I completed it by shading in a section with what I believed to be my score out of 10 in a 'sub-factor'. After completing the re-test, I compared my scores to my baseline data and measured if I had made any improvement.
3

CAUSE	EFFECT
Easy to complete having done it before.	Can easily measure the before and after figures to see if you have improved and reached your long-term goal.
Using the PPW as a re-test allows you to measure progress in a range of 'sub-factors'.	Can measure progress in identified weakness and also identify new areas for development and start the cycle of analysis again to develop whole performance.
Easy to interpret results.	Did not make any mistakes and therefore made more valid comparisons.

4 a It would be ineffective because feeling lower in confidence means they may view their capabilities in a lesser light than they normally would. This means they will score themselves lower and have an inaccurate comparison with a score given previously when they were in a more confident mood.
   b It would be ineffective because the performer gives their opinion in a qualitative method and they may lie to try to impress their coach. This means they may not have made the progress they claimed they had and their result would be inaccurate.
5 a It is important because the coach can check the results and see if they match up with what they believe to be the performer's capabilities.
   b This means it will be more accurate as the performer is getting a second opinion from a more experienced and knowledgeable person whom they trust.

TASK 56 Evaluating the different parts of the PDP

1, 2

PDP DESIGN	APPROACHES	OTHER
Progressing the time of my interval training sessions from 20 minutes in session 4 to 23 minutes in session 5 was an effective part of my PDP.	Using the shadow practice in session 1 of my PDP was very effective because it suited me being at the cognitive stage of learning.	Choosing to do visualisation at the training ground when doing it for the first time was an ineffective part of my PDP.

PDP DESIGN	APPROACHES	OTHER
My PDP was effective due to it having a variety of approaches.		

3. Progressing the time of my interval training sessions from 20 minutes in session 4 to 23 minutes in session 5 was an effective part of my PDP. This was effective because I felt that 20 minutes was too easy so by increasing the time, I continued to feel challenged in session 4. This resulted in me working in my targeted heart rate training zones for longer and my CRE improving rather than hitting a plateau. My PDP was effective due to it having a variety of approaches. This was effective because I never got bored doing the same thing over and over again and therefore I remained motivated. This resulted in me looking forward to going to training and then giving my maximum in every session to improve.

Using the shadow practice in session 1 of my PDP was very effective because it suited me being at the cognitive stage of learning. This was effective because it allowed me to practise without any additional pressure of hitting the shuttle or seeing where it landed. This resulted in me being able to stay calm and fully focused on each of my repetitions and building my muscle memory correctly. Choosing to do visualisation at the training ground when doing it for the first time was an ineffective part of my PDP. This was ineffective because I found myself being distracted by others, like my teammates who were messing around. This resulted in me being unable to produce a vivid image in my head before I stepped on to the training pitch and my confidence levels remained low.

TASK 57 Next steps

1. This pupil should do two things as part of their next steps:
   a. Having identified concentration as a new weakness, they may want to obtain further data on where and when this is a weakness before creating a new PDP to develop it.
   b. Having noted that deep breathing works for them, any PDP they do create to improve their concentration should include this approach as it is also relevant for developing a performer's focus.

EXAM-STYLE QUESTIONS

1. A performer should monitor their progress in the physical factor because it will allow them to see if they are reaching their short-term goals in each session. This means that if they fall short of reaching their goal, they can reduce the intensity of their next interval training session by making the rest period longer.

   A performer should also monitor their progress in the physical factor because they can see if the approaches they are using have worked. This means that they can adapt how they complete interval training in the next session by adding in a skill element if they found the previous session boring.

   Finally, a performer should monitor their progress in the physical factor because it allows them to make comparisons between their halfway re-test and their baseline data. This means they can measure how much their CRE has improved and take a motivation boost from it to continue working hard for the remainder of their PDP.

2. I used the training diary to monitor my progress in the social factor. The training diary was set out as a booklet with a page devoted to every session. On the page, there was space for me to write my short-term goal, session details, thoughts and feelings and my next steps. I took my training diary to training with me and completed it immediately after each session by writing in the session details and how I thought it went. I then finished by writing down my next steps and setting a short-term goal for my next session.

3. It is important that you complete the training diary immediately after each session. This is because you will actually be experiencing the thoughts of how the session went in your head at the time of writing. This means that your answers will be more accurate and can help you set the correct next steps.

    It is important that you ask your coach to check over your diary entries. This is because it can give a different viewpoint as they can check it against how well they thought you did in the session. This means your entries will be more reliable due to you getting input from a more experienced person as the accuracy of your notes is discussed and confirmed.

4. An effective part of my emotional PDP was that I used a variety of approaches. This was effective because I never got bored doing visualisation over and over again and I remained motivated. This resulted in me looking forward to doing something different at each session and really concentrating on achieving my short-term goals.

    An effective part of my emotional PDP was opting to use approaches such as visualisation and deep breathing as they require no equipment. This was effective because I was able to get straight into using these approaches during the session rather than setting things up. This resulted in me learning how to use these approaches quickly and then progressing them into game situations.

    An ineffective part of my emotional PDP was that I first tried visualisation with the TV on at home. This was ineffective because I got distracted by the sounds of the TV as I had not yet mastered the concept of using the approach. This resulted in me wasting a session as I made no progress in it and got frustrated at my inability to focus.

Chapter 10 Answers: Scenario

TASK 58 Mental scenario: script

1. This performer was anxious throughout their performance in tennis due to their friends watching them. This possibly meant that they experienced a lot of negative thoughts about letting them down and losing in front of them. As a result, they may have found themselves playing safe shots down the middle of the court so they did not make mistakes which would have given their opponent the initiative to dictate rallies and win points.

   The performer's anxiety levels may also have led to them experiencing muscular tension when serving. This would have led to their movements being slow and rigid when performing the serve. As a result, their serve would have lacked power and may have hit the net, resulting in more double faults.

   The performer also struggled to concentrate during their performance. This means they could have taken their eye off the ball when they were lining up a smash at the net. This would then have resulted in the timing of their movements being off and making poor contact on the ball and it landing out.

   Finally, the performer made a number of bad decisions which could have impacted their ability during rallies. This may have meant that when their opponent was at the back of the court, they opted against playing a drop shot into the space at the front of the court. As a result, they chose the wrong option and played the ball to the back of the court, which allowed their opponent to stay in the rally.

2. In the future, this performer should learn how to use deep breathing to help control their anxieties. They should initially do this approach at home on their own with all electronic devices turned off. They should then lie down and breathe in through their nose for 4 seconds and out through their mouth for 4 seconds. This would count as one rep and they should repeat this four times. As time goes on, they should progress the approach by reducing the number of reps they perform.

TASK 59 Emotional scenario: bar chart

1. Having completed their emotional PDP, the pupil's ability to control their anger has got a lot worse. This is because they have dropped from 5/10 to 1/10. This means that in football matches, they fail to control their anger when an opponent is getting the better of them. As a result, they then get angry and commit a foul on them and receive a yellow card.

   The fact that controlling their anger has got worse leads to them getting frustrated when a referee makes a decision they disagree with. This results in them shouting and swearing at the referee and being sent off.

   Finally, this increasing inability to control their anger leads to them failing to control their anger when their teammate does not pass to them when they are in a good position to score. This then results in them shouting and criticising their teammate. As a result, both players start to argue rather than track back and fulfil their defensive responsibilities, leaving their defending teammates short.

   Having completed their PDP, their ability to control their fear has also got a lot worse. This is because they have dropped from 4/10 to 1/10. This means that when there is a 50/50 tackle in the middle of the park, they are scared to make the challenge in case of getting injured. This then results in them pulling out of the tackle and this allows their opponent to gain easy possession of the ball. However, their emotional PDP has had a positive impact on their confidence levels. This is because their confidence level has increased from 3/10 to 8/10. This means that when they are playing, they fully believe in their ability to execute more risky passes when in possession. This results in them playing more defensive splitting passes to get their attacking teammates in behind the opposition defence. As a result, their team creates more goal-scoring chances in games.

The fact that their confidence levels have increased has seen them volunteer to take on penalty-taking responsibilities. This is because they fully believe in their ability to score against the goalkeeper and take on board the weight of responsibility of their teammates. This results in them striking their penalty with conviction without changing their mind on where they will place the ball in order to score. As well as this, their emotional PDP has had a positive impact on their resilience. This is because their score has increased from 2/10 to 8/10. This means that they are able to bounce back after missing an easy goal-scoring chance. This results in them forgetting the miss rather than dwelling on it and continuing to make attacking runs into the box before eventually scoring to make up for their earlier miss.

2   Based on their emotional re-test results, this pupil's next steps would be to gather more specific data on their inability to control their anger and fear. This means they will be able to find out the exact causes of both of these weaknesses in order to create a more specific and appropriate PDP.

TASK 60 Social scenario: data collection results

1   A performer may have answered true to getting on with other members of their team because their team's dynamics are very high. This means that they get on very well with one another and support each other in good and bad moments. When playing handball, the performer's teammates may support and encourage them when they miss an easy chance to score because they get on with them. As a result, the performer remains confident and motivated to keep working their hardest as they know their teammates back them.

Another reason why they have answered true to this is because their high levels of team dynamics often see them put their teammates first. When their team was awarded a penalty shot in handball, the performer opted to let the team's pivot take the shot, despite them being the nominated taker, because they got on with them and wanted them to succeed. This resulted in the pivot scoring and getting a confidence boost.

A performer may have answered false to 'I can verbally express myself during a performance because their communication skills are poor. This means that when they are in space in handball and their teammate has the ball, they fail to call for a pass. This leads to their teammate being unaware of their availability, holding on to the ball and being pressured into a mistake to give possession away.

A performer may also have answered false to 'I can verbally express myself during a performance' because their communication skills are poor in other sporting situations. In volleyball, for example, they may not call their name when the ball is about to land between them and their teammate. This means that both players go for the ball as they are unaware of who is going for it and collide with one another. This results in a poor dig being played and the rally being lost.

Finally, a performer may have answered true to showing respect towards opposition players because they demonstrate high levels of etiquette. This means that when an opposition player has fallen after performing a drop shot, the performer will ask if they are OK and offer them their hand to help them up. This results in the opponent appreciating their kindness and the game being played in a respectful manner.

2. A performer will consider the weaknesses identified in their social data collection results when planning a PDP. This means they will then include approaches that are specific to their weaknesses in their PDP to help improve their performance.

A performer will consider using a variety of social approaches when planning their PDP. This means that they will not get bored of doing the same thing and will remain motivated to attend and work hard at training.

A performer will consider partnering with a range of different teammates when planning a social PDP. This means they will be able to get to know all of their teammates and build relationships with everybody, which will further aid their performance on court regardless of their team's starting line-up.

TASK 61 Physical scenario

1. This statement is very true. A performer who has low CRE levels will tire in the final moments of a performance and this can cause lots of different negative impacts.

In badminton, low CRE levels will see the performer unable to keep up with the pace of play. This means that as their opponent plays shots into different areas of the court, they will be too tired to move and reach the shot. This will result in them losing rallies as their opponent picks up on this to keep putting the shuttle into different spaces.

In addition, low CRE levels will see the performer's skill level drop. This means that as they start to tire, they will not be hitting overhead clears with as much power. This will result in shots hanging high at the net for their opponent to punish them with smashes.

Low CRE levels can also see the performer's ability to concentrate decline. This means that they will lose focus when tracking the shuttle and may not move into position early enough. This may result in them being off balance and making a poor contact, which sees their shot hit the net.

As a performer's CRE levels drop, they will also see their ability to make good decisions go down. This means that they will be so tired that they will start to make the wrong shot choices and, rather than play the shot into space, they will play it straight at their opponent. This then results in the performer having time to pick their spot on the court and take the initiative in the rally to win more points.

Finally, a performer who is tired will see their reaction time drop. This means that when an opponent's shot is struck with force directly towards the performer's body, they will be too slow to react and adjust their body. This results in them not being able to manoeuvre their body in time to return the shot and they will lose another rally.

2. The performer should collect data before starting a physical PDP because it will enable them to identify their strengths and weaknesses. This means they can create an appropriate PDP by including relevant approaches to develop their weakness. The performer should also collect data before starting a PDP because it will give them a baseline measurement. This means that when they do the bleep test re-test, the performer can compare their results to measure how much they have improved. Finally, the performer should collect data before starting a physical PDP because it will help them set realistic goals for their PDP. This means that by setting a long-term goal to the next NORM up for the bleep test, the performer will get a motivation boost, which will make them work harder in training to improve.

Answers: Revision paper 1

Section 1

1   a   A performer could receive verbal feedback from a knowledgeable other such as a coach during their physical development plan.
        When developing the smash in badminton, their coach may tell them their strong and weaker sub-routines of the smash during a session. They would tell them this information immediately after each shot. The coach would outline their positives before the negatives. They would tell them why something was good and how to improve a certain area of their performance. This information would be provided in short and sharp bursts.
    b   It is important that feedback is provided immediately after practising the smash during repetition drills. This is because the performance would be fresh in the performer's head, which would help them understand what their coach was saying needed to be improved, which would then lead to them making the appropriate changes to their smash in the next set of repetition drills.
        It is also important that positive feedback is provided before negative feedback. This is because the performer would receive a confidence and motivation boost in hearing something good about their performance, which would make them more likely to listen to what the coach is advising they need to improve in their weaker areas, which would allow them to take it on board and improve their smash.
        Finally, it is important that the coach provides feedback that states why a part of their smash was good. This is because it would be very specific and help the performer to keep on performing this sub-routine to ensure that this aspect of their smash continued to be performed to a high level.

2   a   A performer should collect data before starting a mental development plan because it helps them identify their mental strengths and weaknesses. This means the performer would be able to create a personal development plan to an appropriate weakness, which would make it worthwhile. Also, by knowing their mental weaknesses, it would allow the performer to select and include relevant approaches in their personal development plan to ensure it was specific to their needs.
        A performer should also collect data before starting a mental development plan because it gives them a baseline measurement of their mental performance. This means the performer will have a starting point that they can refer back to in future re-tests to measure improvements and determine whether the plan was working or not.
        Finally, a performer should collect data before starting a mental development plan because it will help them set goals for their mental development plan. This means that by knowing their actual levels of, say, anxiety based on their score from the SCAT test, the performer will be able to set a long-term goal that is realistic to their development in order to boost their motivation.
    b   In the performance profiling wheel (PPW), a performer scored a low 1/10 for their concentration levels. This was poor as when trying to man-mark in basketball, the performer was distracted by the movements of others and stopped tracking their man. This was poor as their man would have been in space under the basket when going for an uncontested rebound and they scored.
        In the PPW, a performer scored a low 1/10 for controlling their anxieties. This was poor as when taking a putt in golf, they started experiencing the shakes.

This was poor as when taking the putt, their hands were shaking so much that they hit the ball with the wrong part of the putter and missed to lose the hole. In the PPW, a performer scored a high 10/10 for mental toughness. This was good as when entering the last lap of their 1500m race in first place, they kept gritting their teeth and pushed through despite their muscles aching. This was good as they maintained their pace and stayed ahead of the other competitors to win. Finally, in the PPW, a performer scored 10/10 for their decision making. This was good as when in a backcourt rally in tennis, they decided to exploit the space at the front of the court with a sliced drop shot. This was good as their opponent did not reach the ball before it bounced twice due to the backspin and the performer won the point.

3 a Co-operation can help a performer develop their smash during a repetition drill in badminton. This means their partner would co-operate by accurately feeding the shuttle to the performer time and again to provide them with opportunities to develop their smash and build up the necessary muscle memory.

This co-operation could also be extended by the partner taking the time to provide the performer with feedback on their progress in the session. This means the partner could provide accurate and informative feedback to help the performer develop identified weaker areas of their smash.

Showing etiquette could help a teammate when trying to develop their control of their fears while using deep breathing. This means that their teammates would respect their training by not trying to embarrass them and remaining silent to help their teammate fully focus on using deep breathing correctly in order to control their fears.

Team dynamics could help a performer when they are struggling to develop their smash during a conditioned game. This means their 'opponent' would encourage and support their teammate when they are struggling and compliment them when they perform the smash to keep their confidence and resilience high during training.

b i A performer may increase their group from six people to eight people when trying to develop communication in the human knot.

A performer may change the people in their group from people who play similar positions to people from other positions when trying to develop team dynamics in the human knot.

ii The performer may increase their group from six to eight people in the human knot because it will make the Human Knot harder. This means that they will have to untangle even more arms, which means they will have to communicate and work more with others in order to be successful.

The performer may change the people in their human knot to players from their position (defenders) to other positions (attackers) on the team. This means the performer will be able to build relationships with all players in their team, which can help them when needing to communicate and work with a player who is perhaps playing out of position beside them in defence to ensure the team's performance remains highly organised.

4 a We should set short-term goals during a development plan because it gives each session a specific focus. This means we can fully focus on the emotional area we are looking to improve in the session and not be side-tracked by anything else, which will increase our chances of improving our performance. We should also set goals during a development plan because they help us track our progress from session to session. This means that if we see ourselves reaching each session's short-term goal, it can stimulate us to keep raising the difficulty of our goals to help ensure we never hit a plateau.

Finally, we should set short-term goals during our emotional development plan because it can motivate us if they are realistic. This means that we will give

100% both in and outside of training to help improve our control of our fears as we know that should we work hard, improvements will be within our reach.

   b A performer may consider the SMART acronym when setting goals for the emotional factor.
      They may consider the term specific by stating what exact situation they want to control their anger in during a football match as part of a long-term goal.
      They may consider the term measurable by including figures they wish to achieve when re-testing the sport emotion questionnaire as part of a long-term goal.
      They may consider adjusting their long-term goal in case of injury or illness occurring at some part of their development plan and them missing training.
      They may consider the term realistic by setting a long-term goal that is not too difficult or too easy for their sport emotion questionnaire re-test based on what they obtained in their baseline test.
      Finally, they may consider the term time-bound by stating the date/point (end of development plan) they wish to achieve their emotional long-term goal by.

Section 2

Factor 1: Social

Factor 2: Emotional

5 a An approach I used during my social development plan was team-building games, e.g. the human knot.
      This consisted of six of us forming a circle and grabbing someone's hand who was not directly next to us. We then did the same with the other hand and also did not grab the same person as the first time. We then tried to untangle ourselves without breaking links/hands at any point while communicating with one another.
   b We used team-building games because they required no equipment and could be done practically anywhere where there was a space. This meant we wasted no time setting things up and were able to spend the full training time concentrating on developing our social factors while trying to untangle the human knot, then progressing it.
      We also used team-building games because they contained a problem to be solved. This meant it forced us to communicate with one another in order to untangle ourselves, which specifically suited the goal of trying to develop our communication.

6 a An approach I used during my emotional development plan was deep breathing.
      I initially carried out deep breathing at home on my own with all electronic devices switched off. I lay flat on my back and closed my eyes. I then breathed in through my nose for a count of 4 seconds, held it for 2 seconds, then breathed out through my mouth for 4 seconds. I repeated this four more times.
   b I used deep breathing because it was a practical approach that can be used anywhere. This meant I was able to use it at home initially to build up my confidence, then, once I'd mastered it, to progress into game situations where I was getting angry.
      I also used deep breathing because a range of elite-level athletes such as Cristiano Ronaldo and Andy Murray use it during high-pressure situations to control their fears. This meant I fully trusted this approach, took it seriously and used it correctly to help control my fears when taking penalties in football.

Section 3

7 a SOCIAL: This performer did very well in the social factor and this is clearly a strength of their performance.
      Being part of a 'tight knit and supportive group' suggests that they are part of a team with very good team dynamics. This was evident in football when the performer missed an easy one-on-one with the goalkeeper. This was good

because their teammates continued to support and encourage them rather than being critical of them. This was then good because the performer remained resilient and continued to make the same attacking runs and eventually scored due to the backing they received from their teammates.

The performer had good etiquette during the match, which is suggested by 'showed respect to … opponents'. This was evident during the football match when the performer had the ball and noticed an opponent down injured. This was good because they sportingly kicked the ball out of play for the opponent to receive treatment. This was then good as their opponent got the treatment they needed and the respect grew between the two sides in a fairly played match.

'Teammates were always aware of where you are based on your loud voice' suggests that the performer had excellent communication skills. This was evident when they were in space on an attack and their teammate had possession. This was good because they shouted their teammate's name loudly to alert them to their open position on the pitch. This was good because it caused their teammate to look up, spot them and pass them the ball to maintain possession.

EMOTIONAL: 'You appeared to be scared … throughout your performance' suggests that the performer was poor at controlling their fears. This inability to control their fears was evident during a backcourt rally in tennis when the performer continued to play safe and hit the ball straight back to their opponent as they were worried about making a mistake. This was poor because rather than making them move, the performer let the opponent dictate the pace of play. This was then poor because the performer was wasting lots of energy chasing shots and eventually did not reach one in the corner and lost the rally.

'Appeared to get frustrated when things were not going your way' suggests that the performer was really poor at controlling their anger. This was evident in tennis when they got annoyed at themselves for hitting a double fault. This was poor as they started smashing their racquet and tried to then take all of their anger out on the next serve. This was then poor as they hit the serve with far too much power and it went out at the back of the court, which resulted in them making another fault. This anger was also evident when the umpire made a decision they disagreed with on a line call. This was poor as they reacted angrily by approaching the umpire and swearing at them several times. This was poor as they were deducted a point for dissent.

b The performer should continue to use a social approach like team building games, e.g. blindfold obstacle race, with their teammates once a week due to it already being a strength. This means they will continue to maintain the high levels of social factors their team already has as they will have opportunities to communicate and build relationships with one another in fun tasks. There is no need to do any more, however, as it is not a weak point.

However, the performer really needs to work on their emotional factors. Their next step should be to collect data on their emotional performance by using a performance profiling wheel (PPW). This means they can get an overview of their biggest emotional strengths and weaknesses, which can then help them decide what to do next. Having done this, the performer should use a specific data-gathering method for their biggest emotional weakness. For example, they may use a disciplinary record for anger. This means they will be able to see what is triggering their anger and fully understand exactly where and why they are getting angry. This could then lead the performer to set very specific goals by including the exact contexts they get angry in, which can really give their emotional development plan a focus. With such a focus, it means they can then select relevant approaches such as deep breathing that are actually compatible with developing control of anger.

Answers: Revision paper 2

Section 1

1. **a** An analytical tool I used to investigate my performance levels in the physical factor was the performance profiling wheel (PPW).
   The PPW was a circle that was divided into 8 different sections. In each section were 10 segments ranging from 1 being weak to 10 being strong. On the outside of each section, I wrote down a physical factor. I carried this out at home on my own with all distractions turned off. I considered my score out of 10 for each physical factor and coloured in that number of segments in that section. After completing this, I identified my biggest physical strength and my biggest physical weakness.
   b A performer might use quantitative data for physical factors because it is a fact that is free from bias opinion. This means the result will be accurate and can be trusted, which can then help a performer actually go away and create a PDP for their weaknesses. With them having accurate data on their physical levels, they can also set their approaches at the correct intensities during their PDP to help them improve.
2. **a** It is important to monitor progress in the social factor because it lets you see if your PDP is actually working. This means that by noting down your thoughts and feelings after each session, you can assess whether that session was effective, then set the appropriate next steps for your next session.
   It is also important to evaluate your progress in the social factor because it lets you compare your baseline and re-test results. This means you can evaluate whether your PDP was successful or not and extend it further if you find you have not yet reached the long-term goal of your plan.
   Finally, it is important to evaluate your progress in the social factor because it lets you identify new weaknesses. This means that you can then take this new weakness through the cycle of analysis and start by collecting data to find out why it is a weakness before creating a relevant PDP to improve it.
   b A method I used to record my progress in social factors was a training diary. The training diary was a booklet that had a page for each session. On each page, there was a space for me to write my short-term goal, what I did in the session, how I thought the session went and what I planned to do next. I completed the training diary immediately after each session. I started by setting my short-term goal for the session. The short-term goal was set based on how the previous session went. I then wrote a description of the approaches I used in the session, e.g. team-building games. I then wrote down how I thought the session went and identified the positives and negatives of the session. Based on this, I then identified what I would do in the next session and whether I would progress it or make it easier.
3. **a** Failing to control my anger was very poor in football when the referee made a decision I disagreed with. This was very poor because I got so frustrated that I shouted and swore at them. This was then very poor because they sent me off.

Failing to control my anger was also very poor in football when my opponent made a bad tackle on me. This was very poor because I got so annoyed that I got up and pushed them. This was then very poor because the referee booked me and I had to watch all of my tackles later in the game so as not to get another yellow card.

Controlling my fears was very good before taking a match-deciding free throw in basketball. This was very good because I managed to stay calm, which helped my muscles stay relaxed. This was then very good as movements were smooth and fluid, which led to my throw being accurate and me scoring.

Being resilient was also very good after I missed an easy smash in badminton. This was very good because I bounced back and did not let that bad miss play on my mind. This was then very good because the next time I had an opportunity to hit a smash, I still went for it and hit an accurate and powerful one to help me win the rally.

Having high levels of confidence was very good for my performance in an offensive one vs one in rugby. This was very good because I felt very positive about my abilities and took the risk of throwing in a fake to pass when approaching my opponent. This was then very good because they were fooled by my fake, which created space for me to break through and reach the try line.

b Failing to control your anger can lead to a drop in your teammates' CRE levels in football. This means that if your team was losing and you then got so angry that you put in a dangerous tackle on an opponent and got sent off, your team would be a player down. This would then lead to them having to work harder to cover extra space, which means they would tire quicker and could concede a goal later in the match when they are exhausted.

Failing to trust your teammates can lead to inappropriate decisions being made in basketball. This means that if you do not rate your teammate and do not trust them to score an easy lay-up, you may ignore them when they are in space close to the basket on a fast break. This then leads to you deciding to take the difficult option of trying to go yourself and beat the opponent, which can lead to you being dispossessed and you losing the chance to score.

Having a lack of confidence can link to relationships breaking down in handball. This means that by not believing in your abilities, you may not show for passes when your teammate is being closed down when in possession. This can then lead to your teammate falling out with you and criticising you for not helping them, which can lead to arguments breaking out on court.

4 a Being able to concentrate can help develop your performance of the smash during repetition drills. This means that by being able to focus on the feedback your partner is giving you on your weak sub-routine, you can then take this on board and put all your efforts into improving this weaker area in your next set and improving your smash.

Being mentally tough can help you during the final set of sprints during interval training. This means that even though you are tired and you want to give up, you push through the tiredness and lactic acid to complete this final set, which can lead to your CRE improving.

I carried out visualisation at home on my own the night before a big match. I turned off all electronic devices and lay down on my bed in complete darkness. I visualised myself scoring a high-pressure free kick in football. In the vision, I included all of the senses, such as the sight of the opposition wall and the sound of the referee's whistle. I then imagined all of my teammates congratulating me when I scored and the positive feeling I had. I repeated this vision in my head five more times. Having done this, I cut down the number of visions I had in my next session to four.

Section 2

PDP 1: Mental factors (anxiety)

PDP 2: Physical factors (accuracy of smash)

5 a I considered including the principle of variety in my mental PDP by using a range of different approaches. This meant I knew I would keep things interesting by mixing things up from session to session, which would lead to my motivation staying high and me giving my all in every session.
I also considered the principle of progression in my mental PDP. This meant that I knew to progress my mental approaches by reducing the number of reps in visualisation so that I could use the approach in game situations where I would have less time to get relaxed in the heat of high-pressure moments.
   b I decided to change the location of my deep breathing after I mastered it in the house on my own to the training ground, where teammates would be around me.
I also decided to change my approach from progressive muscular relaxation to deep breathing when I found it was not working for me.
   c I changed my approach when I found it was not working for me because I was starting to get down and annoyed that my anxieties were not going away. This meant that by changing approach, I took myself out of a negative mindset, which helped me focus on doing an approach that I found to be helpful in controlling my anxieties.
6 a I considered the principle of specificity in my physical PDP by selecting approaches that were specific to my stage of learning. This meant that I decided to use shadow practices at the cognitive stage of learning so that I could learn the very basics of the movements of the smash without any pressure, which suited my beginner stage.
I also considered the principle of excitement during my physical PDP by including fun games at the end of each session. This meant that I knew I had something fun to look forward to during the boring aspects of my approaches, which helped keep me motivated to keep working hard as I knew there would be something good to come in my session.
   b I decided to change my training partner during conditioned games after I got heavily defeated in one session.
I decided to lower my long-term goal after I missed one week of training with the flu.
   c I decided to lower my long-term goal after missing a week of training with the flu. This meant that I ensured my long-term goal remained realistic to my ability levels as I had plateaued slightly after missing a week of training and would not be on the same path that I would have been had I not missed any sessions.

Section 3

7 a PHYSICAL: The performer may have seen their performance levels grow between the baseline and midway re-test because they were progressing the time of each skill session. This would mean that they would have been practising the skill for longer, which would lead to them further grooving the skill and their performance improving.

The performer may have seen their performance levels plateau between the midway and final re-tests because they got injured. This would mean that they would have missed sessions which would have led to their performance levels staying at the same level and not improving any more as they were not getting opportunities to practise and progress their smash.

MENTAL: The performer may have seen the control of their anxieties improve between the baseline and midway re-test because they would have been carrying out approaches such as deep breathing at home on their own. This would mean that they could really focus on performing the approach without anyone judging them, which would have led to them mastering the approach in a calm environment and therefore developing control of their anxieties.

The performer may have seen the control of their anxieties continue to improve between the midway and final re-tests because they would have progressed their approach. This would mean that by decreasing the number of reps they were doing in deep breathing, they would have been getting calmer quicker, which would have led to their performance improving in actual game-like scenarios, where there is not a lot of time to get relaxed in the heat of the moment.

b PHYSICAL: Although the performer's smash was good on some occasions, it was not good on other occasions as they did not perform all of the sub-routines correctly consistently.

The accuracy of the performer's smash was sometimes good in badminton. This was sometimes good as on one occasion they really snapped their wrist on contact and got the shuttle to travel down to the ground quickly. This was good because their opponent did not reach the smash in time and the performer won the rally.

However, the accuracy of the performer's smash was sometimes poor in badminton. This was poor as sometimes they did not track the flight of the shuttle correctly. This was poor as they failed to move their feet or get into position correctly, which led to them attempting the smash while off balance and hitting the net.

MENTAL: The performer's control of their anxieties was very good in a range of different high-pressure situations at the end of their PDP.

Their control of their anxieties was very good just before stepping on to court in a school badminton final. This was very good because they experienced no negative thoughts and had no doubts about their ability as the game started. This was very good because they played freely and attempted more difficult shots, such as a deceptive drop shot when their opponent was at the back of the court to catch them out and win the first rally.

Their control of their anxieties was very good just before serving to stay in the first set of a badminton match. This was very good because their muscles were still relaxed and their movements very smooth and fluid. This was then very good as they got enough power into their high serve, which forced their opponent to the back of the service box and put them under enough pressure that they hit the net with their return.

Index

A
accuracy 12, 23, 59, 91
active learning 116
anger 15–16, 45, 87
anxiety 11–12, 53, 123
approaches
  deep breathing 64–7
  interval training 74–6
  shadow practice 56, 77–9
  team-building games 70–3
  unopposed practice 79–81
  visualisation 68–70
associative stage of learning 58–9
autonomous stage of learning 58–9

B
badminton 12, 20, 40, 57
basketball 12, 22, 42, 50
Biles, Simone 45
bleep test 39–40, 54
boredom 56, 59
Brady, Tom 45

C
cardio-respiratory endurance (CRE) 24, 39, 57, 74, 86
cognitive impacts 11
cognitive stage of learning 58–9
command words 5–7
communication 19–20, 45, 88–9
communication observation schedule 37–8
concentration 12, 45, 85, 123
conditioned game 59
confidence 16–17, 45–6, 50, 68, 70
co-operation 89–90
co-operative learning 112–15
cycle of analysis 29

D
dancing 50, 57
  and trust 19
data
  analysis 53–4
  collection methods 29–44
  model performers 44–6
  qualitative 31, 33, 100
  quantitative 31, 40, 42
  see also feedback
decision making 13–14, 59
deep breathing 64–7
digital analysis 42–4

E
endurance
  muscular 39, 92
  see also cardio-respiratory endurance (CRE)
Ennis-Hill, Jessica 68
etiquette 20–1
evaluation 95–6, 99–103
exam structure 2
exclusion 23
extrinsic feedback 49–50, 59

F
factors impacting performance 9–10
  accuracy 12, 23, 59, 91
  anger 15–16, 45, 87
  anxiety 11–12, 53, 123
  cardio-respiratory endurance (CRE) 24
  cognitive impacts 11
  communication 19–20, 45, 88–9
  concentration 12, 45, 85, 123
  confidence 16–17, 45–6, 50, 68, 70
  decision making 13–14
  emotional 15–19, 35–7, 45, 63, 68–70, 87–8
  etiquette 20–1
  inclusion 22–3
  mental 11–15, 33–5, 45, 63–7, 85–6
  motivation 50, 86
  muscular endurance 92
  physical 23–6, 39–44, 45, 63, 74–81, 91–2
  power 25–6, 45
  problem solving 14–15
  resilience 17–18, 45, 87–8
  social 19–23, 37–8, 45, 63, 70–3, 88–90
  somatic impacts 11
  team dynamics 21–2
  trust 18–19
  width 25
Farah, Mo 17
feedback

extrinsic   49–50, 59
intrinsic   49–50, 59
kinaesthetic   49–50, 59
stages of learning   59
thoughts and feelings   49–50
verbal   49–50
video   49–50
written   49–50
focus   85
  see also concentration
football   50, 57
  and confidence   16
  decision making   13
  etiquette   20
  and motivation   86
  team dynamics   21–2
  and trust   18
  unopposed practice   80
  width   25
frustration   15, 87

G
general observation schedule (GOS)   40–2
goal setting   54–5, 59
  SMART goals   55
golf   50
  problem solving   14–15
Google Maps   114
gymnastics   57

H
handball   21, 50
heptathlon   68
homework   112
human knot   71–2

I
inclusion   22–3
interval training   74–6
intrinsic feedback   49–50, 59

K
key planning information   52–3
kinaesthetic feedback   49–50, 59

L
learning
  active   116
  co-operative   112–15
  stages of   57–9
long-term goals   54–5

M
Messi, Lionel   45
model performers   44–6
monitoring   95–9
motivation   50, 86
multi-stage fitness test (MSFT)   39–40, 54
muscular endurance   39, 92

N
Nada, Rafael   21
National Improvement Framework 2020   vi

O
observation schedule see communication
  observation schedule; general observation
  schedule (GOS)
Olympic Games 2012   68
Olympic Games 2016   17
overload   56–7

P
pedagogical approaches   110–17
peer marking   117
performance
  development   84–93
  improvement   63–81
  practical   3
performance profiling wheel (PPW)   31, 33–5, 53
personal development plan (PDP)   29, 52
  data analysis   53–4
  evaluating   95–6, 99–103
  goal setting   54–5
  improving performance   63–81
  key planning information   52–3
  monitoring   95–9
  next steps   103
  principles of effective practice   59–60
  principles of training   56–7
plateau   56–7, 78
power   25–6, 45
practical performance   3
practice
  principles of   59–60
  retrieval   110–11
  see also stages of learning
principles of effective practice   59–60
principles of training   56–7
problem solving   14–15
progression   56, 59

Q
qualitative data 31, 33, 100
quantitative data 31, 40, 42
questionnaire 35–7

R
repetition drills 59
resilience 17–18, 45, 87–8
re-test 99–101
retrieval practice 110–11
reversibility 56
Ronaldo, Cristiano 26, 86
rugby 16, 21, 64

S
scenarios 106–8, 113
shadow practice 59, 77–9
short-term goals 54–5, 59
skills, stages of learning 57–9
SMART goals 55, 59
somatic impacts 11
specificity 56, 59
stages of learning 57–9
standardised fitness test 39–41

T
tactics 42, 79
team-building games 70–3
team dynamics 21–2
tedium 56
tennis 57
  decision making 14
  etiquette 20, 21
  shot placement 14
think-pair-share 116
training diary 97–9
trust 18–19
T-Test 39

U
unopposed practice 79–81

V
variety 59
verbal feedback 49–50
video analysis 31, 42–4, 59
video feedback 49–50
visualisation 68–70

W
width 25
Wilkinson, Jonny 64
Williams, Serena 45
written feedback 49–50

Photo credits

Images reproduced by permission of: **p.14** Daxiao Productions/Adobe Stock; **p.17** PCN Photography/Alamy Stock Photo; **p.19** jeancliclac/Adobe Stock; **p.21** Mauricio Paiz/Alamy Stock Photo; **p.26** *t* Xinhua/Alamy Stock Photo, *b* Xinhua/Alamy Stock Photo; **p.42** dpa picture alliance/Alamy Stock Photo; **p.45** *tl* Tribune Content Agency LLC/Alamy Stock Photo, *tr* ZUMA/Alamy Stock Photo, *bl* Pro Shots/Alamy Stock Photo, *br* Neil Tingle/Alamy Stock Photo; **p.64** REUTERS/Alamy Stock Photo; **p.68** PCN Photography/Alamy Stock Photo; **p.86** Daniele Badolato - Juventus FC/Contributor; **p.97** mizar_21984/Adobe Stock; **p.108** lzf/Adobe Stock; **p.114** True Images/Alamy Stock Photo.

Images on pp. 2, 5, 9, 29, 49, 52, 63, 84, 95, 106, 110 reproduced by permission of Rawpixel.com/Adobe Stock.